# THE DOCTRINE OF THE DIVINE NAME

Program in Judaic Studies
Brown University
BROWN JUDAIC STUDIES
Edited by
Jacob Neusner
Wendell S. Dietrich, Ernest S. Frerichs, William Scott Green,
Calvin Goldscheider, David Hirsch, Alan Zuckerman

**Project Editors (Project)**

David Blumenthal, Emory University (Approaches to Medieval Judaism)
William Brinner (Studies in Judaism and Islam)
Ernest S. Frerichs, Brown University (Dissertations and Monographs)
Lenn Evan Goodman, University of Hawaii (Studies in Medieval Judaism)
William Scott Green, University of Rochester (Approaches to Ancient Judaism)
Norbert Samuelson, Temple University (Jewish Philosophy)
Jonathan Z. Smith, University of Chicago (Studia Philonica)

Number 149
THE DOCTRINE OF THE DIVINE NAME
An Introduction to Classical Kabbalistic Theology

by
Stephen G. Wald

# THE DOCTRINE OF THE DIVINE NAME
An Introduction to Classical Kabbalistic Theology

by
Stephen G. Wald

Scholars Press
Atlanta, Georgia

# THE DOCTRINE OF THE DIVINE NAME
An Introduction to Classical Kabbalistic Theology

© 1988
Brown University

**Library of Congress Cataloging in Publication Data**

Wald, Stephen G.
    The doctrine of the divine name.

    (Brown Judaic studies ; no. 149)
    I. God (Judaism)--Name--History of doctrines.
2. Cabala--History. I. Title. II. Series.
BM610.W35    1988    296.1'6    88-11520

ISBN 1-930675-38-0

Printed in the United States of America
on acid-free paper

**PREFACE**

My primary goal in this study is to present the main elements of kabbalistic thought in a form which is both intelligible and authoritative. The study is built around texts, mostly deriving from the closing decades of the thirteenth century, the crucial period in which kabbalistic thought first coalesced into a fairly coherent and unified intellectual tradition. The centerpiece of the exposition is a detailed analysis of the doctrine of the Divine Name as presented in a text titled *The Secrets of the Letters of the Divine Name* – one of the most complete, systematic, and authoritative presentations of the elements of kabbalistic theology to be found in classical kabbalistic literature.

The text of *The Secrets of the Letters* is difficult, as difficult as any to be found in the entire Zoharic literature. But it is the only text which presents in a systematic way the totality of the Zohar's doctrine of the divine *middot*, or, as they are better known, the *ten sephirot* – their procession one from the other, their metaphysical nature, and their spiritual content.

Because of this text's difficulty it has never before been translated, not even into Hebrew. Moreover, many of the more common printed texts have become corrupted through the negligence or the misunderstanding of the printers. Manuscripts, on the other hand, have preserved much better texts. Similarly, certain printed editions preserve significantly better readings, some of which were based on manuscripts not available to me.

The body of this work includes four parts:
    1) a newly edited Aramaic text of *The Secrets of the Letters* in its entirety (placed at the very end for the use of the Judaica scholar), and

    2) an annotated translation of the systematic section of the *The Secrets of the Letters*, lines 1–334, (approximately one half of the text) with critical notes.

These two sections provide the necessary *critical foundation* for the conceptual analysis.

## PREFACE

The *conceptual analysis*, which is the heart of the book, is divided between the two remaining parts:

> 3) a presentation, preceding the translation, of the essential elements of the Doctrine of the Name in abstract, systematic form, and
>
> 4) a running commentary and paraphrase of the translation, which follows it, including references to those sections of the systematic presentation which are necessary for the proper understanding of any given passage.

The purpose of this analysis is to present the essential contents of kabbalistic theology to the non-expert in a manner which is both authoritative and intelligible. This theology is placed within its proper historical setting in the introduction to the work, and its concrete religious significance within that context is also clarified there.

The work may be read on a number of different levels, depending upon how deeply or how critically one wishes to approach it. The introduction and the systematic section can be read independently of the translation, which fills them out with concrete content. The translation can be read with or without the commentary, which justifies the systematic presentation. Similarly, one who is intimidated by the difficulty of the text can use the commentary as a paraphrase in place of the literal translation. The critical notes and Aramaic text are intended for the scholar who wishes to check my readings and interpretations. Regardless of the level on which the reader approaches this material, I hope my presentation will afford him some glimpse into the intellectual and spiritual riches which this tradition contains.

I wish to express my gratitude to the workers of the Institute of Microfilms of Hebrew Manuscripts at the National and University Library in Jerusalem for their help, and to thank the Curators of the Bodleian Library, Oxford University, and the Library of the Jewish Theological Seminary in New York for their kind permission to publish manuscript material in their possession.

**PREFACE**

I wish to express my appreciation to two scholars who were particularly helpful to me in the course of the composition of this work. The work owes a great deal to the open mindedness and erudition of Professor Moshe Idel of the Hebrew University, who read and criticized several drafts of the work in progress. It also owes much to the interest and advice of Rabbi Gedalia Fleer, whose intimate knowledge of Kabbalah both in theory and in practice have been a constant guide to me in this difficult and obscure area of Jewish lore.

Finally, I want to thank my wife Stephanie, who first introduced me to the world of electronic word-processing and type setting. Without her constant help and advice, it is unlikely that I would ever have managed to finish this work at all.

Stephen Wald<br>Jerusalem 1987

## CONTENTS

| | |
|---|---|
| **Preface** | v |
| **List of Abbreviations** | x |
| | |
| **Introduction** | 1 |
|     The Historical Context of the Zohar | 3 |
|     Maimonides and the Divine Attributes | 7 |
|     The Circle of the Zohar and Maimonidean Metaphysics | 15 |
|     The Circle of the Zohar and Maimonidean Spirituality | 17 |
|     The Elements of the Divine Name | 23 |
| | |
| **Part One: The Concept of the Divine Name** | 33 |
|     Rabbinic Background | 36 |
|     Philosophical Elements | 43 |
|     Synthesis | 49 |
|     Structure and Symbol | 59 |
| | |
| **Part Two: The Secrets of the Letters – Annotated Translation** | 71 |
|     Translation | 73 |
|     Critical Notes | 97 |
| | |
| **Part Three: The Secrets of the Letters – Commentary** | 115 |
| | |
| **Part Four: The Secrets of the Letters – Aramaic Text** | 145 |
| | |
| **Index** | 185 |

## List of Abbreviations and Standard Works Cited

Zohar = Vilna edition, three volumes 1924

MS. O = Oxford Manuscript of the Zohar – MS.Bodl.Or.574

MS. S = Jewish Theological Seminary Manuscript of the Zohar – Mic. 1761

ZC = Zohar Cremona 1558–1560

ZHS = Zohar Hadash Salonika 1597

ZHV = Zohar Hadash Venice 1658

ZHM = Zohar Hadash Munkatch 1911

*Ketem Paz* = commentary of Rabbi Shimon Lavi to Zohar, published on Genesis. Reprint Jerusalem 1981.

SLDN = Secrets of the Letters of the Divine Name. By line number of our edition.

*Book of Creation* – standard edition with commentaries. Reprint Jerusalem 1962.

*Sefer HaBahir* – Hebrew text and translated by Rabbi Aryeh Kaplan, New York 1979.

*Shekel HaKodesh* – edited by A.W. Greenup. London 1911. Reprint Jerusalem 1969.

*Shoshan Eduth, Ten Sephirot* – published by Gershom Scholem under the title "Two Treatises of Moses de Leon" in *Kovets al Yad* (8) Jerusalem.

*Shaare Tsedek* – Cracow 1881. Reprint Jerusalem 1967.

*Shaare Orah* – edited by Joseph ben Shlomo, two volumes. Jerusalem 1970.

MRI = *Mechilta de Rabbi Ishmael*, ed. Horowitz–Rabin.

BR = *Bereishit Rabbah*, ed. Theodor–Albeck.

Mishnah, Talmud, Midrash Rabbah – standard rabbinic editions.

*Pirke Rabbi Eliezer* – ed. R. David Luria. Reprint Jerusalem 1970.

## ABBREVIATIONS

*Mishneh Torah*, "The Book of Knowledge" – ed. R. Saul Lieberman. Jerusalem 1964.

*Guide of the Perplexed* – trans. S. Pines. Chicago 1963.

Maimonides' *Commentary to the Mishnah* – Hebrew translation by R. Joseph Kafih. Jerusalem 1963.

*Studies* = Ephraim Gottlieb, *Studies in the Literature of the Kabbalah*. Tel Aviv 1976.

*Major Trends* = Gershom Scholem, *Major Trends in Jewish Mysticism*. New York 1941.

*Mishnat HaZohar* = I. Tishbi, *Mishnat HaZohar*, 3rd. edition. Jerusalem 1971.

*Grammar* = M. Z. Kadari, *A Grammar of the Aramaic of the Zohar*. Jerusalem 1971.

*Chapters* = Yehuda Liebes, *Chapters from the Zohar Lexicon*. Dissertation, Hebrew University in Jerusalem.

# THE DOCTRINE OF THE DIVINE NAME

## INTRODUCTION

# INTRODUCTION

## The Historical Context of the Zohar

The historical origins of the Kabbalah are as shrouded in mystery as are the main doctrines of its mystical theology. In particular, the central document of the classical Kabbalah, the Zohar, has remained a subject of dispute and controversy among traditional scholars for centuries, and in recent years academic scholars have joined the fray. Some have viewed this enormous body of mystical literature, which claims various teachers of the Mishnah and Talmud as its protagonists, as an authentic document of second century Palestine. They account for the blatantly late material present in the Zohar by ascribing it to editorial additions and modifications of later generations. Others have viewed the work as a total fraud, a gross forgery which brazenly projects its own irrational and superstitious views back into the enlightened world of the authentic Talmudic sages.[1]

Concerning certain facts, however there seems to be a fairly clear consensus. The Zohar first appeared on the stage of Jewish history in the north of Spain during the last few decades of the thirteenth century. It was not known even to the immediately preceding generations of Kabbalists in Spain and southern France, and certainly the Jewish philosophers of the eleventh and twelfth centuries never saw it. Only slowly did its influence spread from the closed esoteric circle of Spanish Kabbalists, until it finally became established in the sixteenth and seventeenth centuries as a canonical text for virtually all of world Jewry, second only to the Talmud itself in holiness and authority.[2]

One additional clue to the mysterious appearance of the Zohar was its close association with the names of two prominent writers of the period, Moses de Leon and Joseph Gikatilia. These two Kabbalists composed numerous tracts which express in clear Hebrew prose many of the very same doctrines which we find in the Zohar itself.

---

[1] For a complete review of this issue see *Mishnat HaZohar* vol. 1 pp.44–66.

[2] See *Mishnat HaZohar* vol. 1 pp. 28–44, and *Or Yakar*, Tikkune Zohar vol. 2 (Jerusalem 1973) p. 104b.

## INTRODUCTION

Starting from this meagre data, Gershom Scholem began some seventy years ago the difficult task of unravelling the various threads of this riddle. In a series of carefully argued scholarly papers, he and his disciples Isaiah Tishbi and Ephraim Gottlieb firmly established a number of conclusions.

### The Circle of the Zohar

First of all, they showed that the connection between the Hebrew writings of Moses de Leon and the Aramaic text of the Zohar go far beyond mere similarity of doctrine and content. A clear literary dependence was established, though the direction of this dependence was at times unclear.[3] A similar literary dependence has been noted between certain parts of the Zohar and the writings of Joseph Gikatilia, especially his works *Shaare Tsedek* and *Shaare Orah*.[4]

Given some firm historical evidence concerning the central role of Moses de Leon in the propagation of the Zohar in Spain, Scholem and his earlier disciples drew the conclusion that Moses de Leon was the author of the Zohar.[5] More recently however, this role has been more cautiously described as that of the "redactor" of the Zohar.[6] The precise relationship of the various Hebrew writings of Moses de Leon to each other is still somewhat unclear.[7] As such, it may be premature to jump to any conclusions concerning the exact relation of his works to the Zohar. The situation regarding the writings of Gikatilia is much the same.[8]

Another problem which Scholem and his disciples addressed was the single or multiple authorship of the text. The Zohar is not a book in the normal sense of the word. It is a "literature," a vast

---

[3] See for example Scholem's paper in *Mada'ai HaYehadut* I (1926) pp. 16–29 and Tishbi's edition of Moses de Leon's kabbalistic responsa, in his *Studies in Kabbalah and its Offshoots*, Jerusalem 1982 pp.36–75.

[4] See Gottlieb, *Studies* p.97.

[5] *Major Trends* pp.190 ff. and *Mishnat HaZohar* vol. 1 p. 28 ff.

[6] *Contemporary Jewish Religious Thought*, New York 1987, p. 639.

[7] See *Mishnat HaZohar* vol 1 pp.105 ff. and Alexander Altmann's introduction to his edition of Moses de Leon's *Or Zarua*, in *Kovets Al Yad*, no. 9 pp. 219–244.

[8] See Gottlieb, *Studies* pp. 96–131.

collection of numerous independent compositions of varying sizes, styles, and literary forms.[9] Some pieces, written in classic midrashic form, follow the dynamic and order of whatever verses they happen to be expounding. Others are vast speculative treatises of mystical theology, organized systematically around the immanent structure of the object of analysis or contemplation. Some have a concrete earthly setting, a clear literary framework, and a familiar cast of characters. Others are wholly anonymous, or open with the mere name of Rabbi Shimon, never to be mentioned again. Some parts expound their content in great detail, using rational theological argumentation, and taking care to explain virtually every obscure point. Others seem to be prophetic exclamations, brief and obscure to the point of nearly total unintelligibility.

Here too, Scholem and his disciples have made considerable progress. Virtually all the various parts of the Zohar have been shown to possess a remarkably high degree of consistency in both doctrine and terminology.[10] This reinforced Scholem's final conclusion that the Zohar was composed by a single author, and that his name was Moses de Leon. However, this theory does not account for the bewildering variety mentioned above, a variety which has led some scholars to posit a multiple authorship for the Zohar, or even to incline toward the traditional notion of the Zohar as the creation of many generations. Scholem himself originally subscribed to this view, and published a work supporting it.[11] Indeed the specific results of his later research are not necessarily inconsistent with the notion of a final harmonizing redaction of earlier material, or of the Zohar as the product of a fairly homogeneous school of kabbalistic thought.

One conclusion emerges unambiguously from the many still obscure and disputed points: the Zohar in its present form represents the most fully developed and authoritative expression of a school of kabbalistic thinking and writing whose most notable historical representatives are Moses de Leon and Joseph Gikatilia. These two Kabbalists were both familiar with the various texts of the Zohar

---

[9] *Major Trends* pp. 159–163 and *Mishnat HaZohar* vol. 1 pp. 17–28.

[10] See Gottlieb, *Studies* pp. 163–214 especially p. 172 note 47.

[11] *Mada'ai HaYehadut* I (1926) pp. 16–29.

literature in their original intellectual and cultural context, and may have been intimately involved in one way or another in their very composition. This school constitutes the immediate context in which the Zohar must be interpreted.

## Theological Context

This question of context is central to the problem of theological interpretation. The texts of the Zohar are highly ambiguous. Even when one can make out the literal sense of a given passage, its larger significance is not always clear. Radically different interpretations of the Zohar's theological content have been given by modern scholars. At one extreme, the symbolic surface of the Zohar has been viewed as barely concealing a purely Neo-Platonic system of ideas and concepts.[12] At the other extreme, it has been viewed as the expression of the most profound and hidden recesses of the Jewish soul, the result of primary-processes which transcend the limitations of ordinary waking consciousness, and which can only be brought to consciousness in their symbolic garb. Any attempt to find rational or intelligible content in these symbols is at best doomed to failure and at worst liable to empty the Kabbalah of all its meaning.[13]

Which of these interpretations is correct? Is there perhaps some third alternative? The answer to these questions ultimately depends upon the context within which one chooses to interpret the text. To a certain extent the entire history of Jewish mysticism presented in Scholem's classic work *Major Trends in Jewish Mysticism* is a grand attempt to construct a context in which the text of the Zohar should be viewed. For Scholem, Kabbalah arises out of an underground stream of gnostic and mythic thinking[14] which represents an unequivocal rejection of orthodox medieval Jewish thought[15] and a

---

[12]See *Major Trends* pp. 208–209.
[13]See *Major Trends* pp. 224–225.
[14]See Scholem, *Origins of the Kabbalah*, 1987, ch. 2.
[15]See *Major Trends* pp. 22–39.

radical alternative to institutionalized rabbinic monotheism.[16] However, a closer examination of the immediate context in which the Zohar appeared reveals clear literary and intellectual ties to the mainstream of medieval Jewish thought on the one hand and to the traditional theologies of classical rabbinic sources on the other which raise grave doubts as to the validity of Scholem's interpretation.

The writings of Moses de Leon and Joseph Gikatilia contain numerous clear programmatic statements in which the general intent and purposes of their kabbalistic doctrines are set forth. In particular, Gikatilia composed an elaborate introduction to his work *Shaare Orah* in which he placed the most fundamental doctrines of Kabbalah into their proper intellectual and religious context. Similarly, Moses de Leon's works *Shekel haKodesh* and *Shoshan Eduth* have important introductory passages. These texts, among others will be considered in detail below. What they all have in common is their clear connection, both in form and substance, to the writings of one of the greatest of all Jewish philosophers, Moses ben Maimon, Maimonides (1135–1204). In order to understand these kabbalistic texts properly we must first examine certain elements of Maimonidean philosophy which seem to have had a particular influence upon the thinking of both Moses de Leon and Joseph Gikatilia.

## Maimonides and the Divine Attributes

Already in the beginning of *Major Trends*, Scholem placed the origins and development of the central doctrine of Kabbalah, the doctrine of the *Sephirot*, in the context of the Maimonidean doctrine of the Divine Attributes. But whereas Scholem felt that this Maimonidean doctrine could be summarized in one sentence and dismissed in the next,[17] the Kabbalists themselves seem to have found this central Maimonidean idea far more interesting and compelling. Moreover, they seem to have grasped the systemic place of this doctrine within Maimonidean thought as a whole. In particular, they seem to have assimilated certain aspects of this

---

[16] See Scholem, *On the Kabbalah and its Symbolism*, New York 1965, pp. 5–11.
[17] See *Major Trends* p. 11.

doctrine into their own doctrine of the *Sephirot*, both with respect to the the mode in which one can know God, and with respect to the role of this knowledge in the positive worship of God on earth.

### Speculative Knowledge as the Foundation of Faith

Maimonides based his entire positive religious system upon speculative knowledge of God. The first commandment which is the religious foundation of all the other commandments is to know that there is a God. This God is not known from history or scripture, but rather He is recognized through the majesty and order of His creation, which He constantly supports and maintains through His infinite creative power.

> [1] The foundation of all fundamental principles and the basis of all the sciences is to know that there is a First Being who maintains all beings in existence, and all beings, from heaven, earth, and that which is between them, came into being only through the reality of His being.
>
> [5] This Being is the God of the world, the Master of all the earth. He governs the sphere with a power that has neither limit nor end, with a power that never ceases – for the sphere turns constantly, and it is not possible for it to turn without One who turns it. He, blessed be He, is the One who turns it, without a hand and without a body. (Mishneh Torah, Foundations ch.1)

The requirement of knowing God as the necessary prerequisite of all religious obligation involves Maimonides in a difficulty, since God cannot, strictly speaking, be known at all.

> [9] . . . The true reality of this matter cannot be grasped or investigated by the human mind. This is what the verse said: "Can you discover the mystery of God? Can you discover the limit of the Almighty?" (Job 11:7) [10] What then is it that Moses our master sought to grasp when he said: "Show me your Glory . . . " (Exodus 33:18) (Ibid)

### The Possibility of Knowing God

The story of Moses' request to see God's Glory (Ex. 33:12–34:8) provides the focal point around which Maimonides discusses the possibility and religious significance of knowing God. He expands upon this subject at great length in his *Guide of the Perplexed* (Part 1, ch. 54):

> Know that the master of all the sages, Moses our master, made two requests, and received a response to both of them. The first request was that he asked Him, may He be exalted, to let him know His essence and true reality. The second request, which he put first, was that He should let him know His attributes. He, may He be exalted, responded to both questions by promising to let him know of all His attributes and that they are His actions, whereas He informed him that His essence could not be grasped as it truly is. . . .

First of all, Maimonides points out that Moses made two different requests of God. The more ambitious aspiration to know God's very essence was answered only in part. It refers to a kind of divine prophetic enlightenment which goes beyond both speech and knowledge. Even though this mystical trend in Maimonidean thought may have also had considerable impact on the development of Kabbalah, it is primarily Moses' more modest request for positive knowledge of God's *ways* which concerns us here.

> Concerning his request to know His attributes, which was expressed in the verse: "Inform me of Your ways that I may know you. etc." (Ex. 33:13), consider what wonders are included in this verse. When he said "Inform me of Your ways that I may know you," this indicates that He, may He be exalted, may be known through His attributes, such that if one were to know the *ways* one would know Him. When he said "so that I might find favor in Your eyes," this indicates that one who knows God is he who *finds favor in His eyes*, not one who only fasts and prays. On the contrary, he who knows Him is the one who is favored and is close [to Him], while he who is ignorant of Him is rejected and distanced [from Him]. Moreover with regard to the extent of the knowledge or ignorance will be the favor or the rejection [by Him], the closeness [to] or the distance [from Him]. But we have digressed from the subject of this chapter, so let me return to it.

### Divine Knowledge as Intimacy and Providence

Maimonides included many important issues in these brief lines. Knowledge of God is a religious concern because it is through knowledge of Him that one draws close to Him. Religious intimacy with God cannot be established with God by mere emotional devotion and self-denial. God who is a spiritual–intellectual Being can only be approached by rising out of the physical world into His own etherial element, i.e. through the exercise of the spiritual-intellectual powers of the mind. Only in this way is prayer in its true inner sense acceptable.

Moreover, this may be a reference to Maimonides' doctrine of individual providence.[18] While Maimonides' true opinion on this issue has been disputed by modern scholars, his *prima facia* position is that God will protect those who know Him from all harm, physical and spiritual, in this world and the next.[19] In this literal sense too, prayer can only answered if one *knows* God. Merely calling out to Him is insufficient. As we shall see below, it is this *prima facia* position which was understood and accepted by Moses de Leon and Joseph Gikatilia.

Maimonides then turns to examine in detail the way in which knowledge of His attributes leads to knowledge of Him:

> When he requested knowledge of His attributes ... then he requested comprehension of His essence, may He be exalted, by saying "Show me Your glory" (Ex. 33:18), he was answered with regard to the first request (which was *Inform me of Your ways*) and was told: "I will cause all of my Goodness to pass before you" (Ex. 33:19), and he was told by way of response to the second question: "You cannot see My face, etc." (Ex. 33:20) Concerning the phrase *all of my Goodness* – this is an allusion to the presentation of all of the existent beings before him, concerning which beings it was said: "And God saw all that He had made, and behold it was very good" (Gen. 1:31). [By saying] that they were to be presented before him, I mean that he was to comprehend their nature and their interconnectedness, one to the other, such that he would comprehend the way in which He governs them both in general and in particular. ... a comprehension of these actions, which are His attributes, may He be exalted, by means of which He may be known.

The *Goodness* which God promised to show Moses in response to his request is identified by Maimonides with the *very good* which God applied to the totality of Creation at its completion on the sixth day. But it was not just a vast array of disconnected phenomena which Moses saw. He grasped their essential interconnectedness, the hierarchy of the infinite chain of being which leads necessarily back

---

[18]Cf. Rabbi Joseph Kafih's Hebrew translation of the *Guide* (Jerusalem 1977) p. 84 note 10.

[19]*Guide* part 3 ch. 51.

to God himself. Moses saw in this infinite chain more than the mere fact that all of reality has its origin in God. He saw also the concrete principles of Wisdom and Goodness by which God *governs* the world.

Maimonides then proceeds to justify this identification:

> The proof that he was promised that he would comprehend His actions, may He be exalted, can be found in the fact that the only thing of which he actually gained knowledge were His attributes of action: *merciful, gracious, slow to anger* (Ex. 34:6-7). It has thus been made clear that the *ways* which he sought to know and of which he gained knowledge were the actions which proceed from Him, may He be exalted. The Sages called them *middot*, and spoke of the *thirteen middot*. According to their usage this term is applied to moral qualities: "There are four middot among those who give charity"; "There are four middot among those who go to the house of learning" (Mishna Avot 5:13-14). There are many [examples of this usage.] The meaning here, however, is not that He possesses moral qualities, but rather that He produces actions which are comparable to those actions which proceed from us with regard to moral qualities, i.e. psychological predispositions, not that He, may He be exalted, possesses psychological predispositions.

Maimonides explains in his ethical writings that visible moral action corresponds to the inner state of the subject's moral character. That character is constantly being shaped by repeated concrete action, while the actions themselves are a direct expression of that inner character.[20] On this model, every specific concrete action corresponds to an inner psychological predisposition. Similarly with God, His concrete visible actions in the world correspond to invisible abstract principles of wisdom and goodness. The concrete order of the physical universe has its ontological roots in the metaphysical order of God's providence, that is in the moral order of His *middot* or attributes.

### Divine Knowledge as Imitatio Dei

Even though God promised to show Moses all of his *goodness*, the answer which Moses received was only a relatively small number of God's moral attributes, i.e. the thirteen attributes of *Mercy*. Maimonides explains next why this was so:

---

[20]Maimonides, *Commentary to Mishnah*, Introduction to *Avot* ch.4.

## INTRODUCTION

> Now the only reason that He limited Himself to mentioning these *thirteen middot*, despite the fact that he grasped *all of His Goodness* – that is all His actions – is that these are the actions which proceed from Him, may He be exalted, with regard to the creation and governance of man. For this was the final aim of his question, as he said at the end of the verse: "that I may know you, so that I might find favor in Your eyes, for behold – this nation is Your people" (Ex. 33:13), [i.e. a people] which I must govern with actions in which I shall imitate Your actions in governing them.

Moses was not merely asking for speculative knowledge for its own sake. His primary concern in seeking this knowledge was a very specific final goal: imitation of God in positive moral activity in the world. After a long digression in which he discusses the various concrete ways in which this human imitation of the divine can be effected, Maimonides returns at the very end of the chapter to reemphasize this crucial point:

> Though we have digressed from the subject of the chapter, we have nevertheless explained the reason why He limited Himself to mentioning only these [thirteen attributes], for they are necessary in the governance of the cities, since the final perfection of man lies in imitation of Him, may He be exalted, to the extent that this is possible, that is to say that we should model our actions on His actions, as they explained while interpreting the verse "You shall be holy" (Lev. 19:2), for they said: "Just as He is gracious, so you too should be gracious; just as He is merciful, so you too should be merciful." (Siphre to Deut. 11:22)

The significance of Maimonides' description of positive moral imitation of God's attributes in the world as the "final perfection of man" should not be underestimated. In the final chapter of the *Guide*, he repeats this claim and places this moral imitation of God even higher than the prophetic enlightenment which seemed to be the goal of the work as a whole. The long term impact of this extremely "Jewish" mystical ideal on the spiritual world of the circle of the Zohar was enormous.

Summary

In summary: The knowledge of God's attributes relates to two primary areas of religious concern. The first is religious awareness and intimacy – *dvekut*, the cleaving of the soul to God through knowledge, love, and fear of Him. A secondary result of this *dvekut* may be individual providence and the answering of prayer in the literal sense. The second area is that of *imitatio dei* – the human imitation of God's positive moral attributes on earth as the final perfection of man.

These two areas of religious concern were incorporated into Maimonides' authoritative religious code, *Mishneh Torah*, in the form of individual commandments. Below, we will see the direct literary impact of these authoritative formulations on Joseph Gikatilia's introduction to *Shaare Orah*. For this reason alone, it is significant to bring them here in full:

> [1] We are commanded to love and to fear this great and awesome God, as it is written: "Thou shalt love the Lord, thy God" (Deut. 6:5), and it is written: "Fear the Lord, thy God" (Deut. 6:13). [2] What is the way to the love of Him and the fear of Him? When man contemplates His mighty and wondrous actions and creations, and sees in them His infinite and incomparable wisdom, immediately he is filled with love and praises and glorifies, and is possessed by an overwhelming desire to know the Great Name, just as King David said: "My soul thirsts for God, the living God." (Foundations, ch. 2)

After the preceding discussion from the Guide, this passage should be fairly clear. The following passages (from *Deot* ch. 1), however, place the second issue, *imitatio dei*, into the context of Maimonides general ethical theory, and require a little background and comment:

> [1] All human beings possess many personal characteristics . . . One man may be a hot head who is constantly angry, while another may be so calm that he never gets anger, or if he does it will only be a little in many years.

Following Aristotle,[21] Maimonides holds that moral virtues become moral vices when they predominate in the human personality to either too great or to too little extent. These extremes of too much and too little constitute antithetical polar opposites, both of which are equally dangerous for the soul. The soul must learn to steer a path of moderation between these two extremes:

---

[21]*Nichomachean Ethics*, Book 2:5–8.

[3] The two extremes of each personal characteristic are not a good path, and it is not proper for a man to walk in them, nor to teach them to himself. . . . [rather] he should walk in the path of the good which is the straight path. [4] The straight path is the moderate measure *(middah)* of each of the many personal characteristic which a man possesses. It is that personal characteristic which is equally distant from each of the two extremes, and which draws close to neither of them.

In line with the discussion in the *Guide* brought above, Maimonides then identifies this proper moderate path with the positive attributes of God:

[5] We are commanded to walk in these moderate ways, which are the good and straight ways, as it is written: "You shall walk in His ways" (Deut. 28:9). [6] This is the interpretation which they learned concerning this commandment: just as He is called gracious, so you too should be gracious; just as He is called merciful, so you too should be merciful; just as He is called holy, so you too should be holy. In this way the prophets called God by all these descriptive terms: *slow to anger, abounding in kindness, righteous, upright, pure, mighty, powerful,* and so on – to let it be known that these are good and straight ways, and that one is obligated to direct himself according to them and to imitate [them] to the extent of his ability.

This notion of *descriptive terms* was developed by both the Zohar and Gikatilia into the centerpiece of their doctrine of the *sephirot*. But whereas for Maimonides all these *descriptive terms* apply to the moderate middle path, the Zohar and Gikatilia divide them up between all three points of Maimonides' scheme: the two polar extremes *and* the middle point.[22] Even though they agree that it is the goal of man to cling to the middle path only,[23] in describing God's attributes they give equal weight to the extremes and assign the various *descriptive terms* to their proper places under three distinct headings: *Kindness, Judgement, and Mercy.* The theological implications of this shift will be discussed below. We can only hope in this work to lay the foundations for an adequate analysis of the kabbalistic ideal of *imitatio dei*.

---

[22]*Shaare Orah* pp. 220–221, 243, and see the commentary to *The Secrets of the Letters*, letter *vav*, the ethical dimension.

[23]*Shekel HaKodesh* p. 53.

## The Circle of the Zohar and Maimonidean Metaphysics

The position of Maimonides which was described above reflects a synthesis of abstract metaphysical and concrete religious concerns. The circle of Kabbalists whose views we will now consider created a similar synthesis, which is highly dependent upon Maimonides in many respects. Broadly speaking, the works of Moses de Leon will provide us with the metaphysical context of their kabbalistic doctrines, while the introduction to Joseph Gikatilia's *Shaare Orah* will provide the religious context.

The following programmatic statement is quite characteristic of Moses de Leon's approach to kabbalistic theology:

> Part One: One should know and comprehend ... that there is no one who can grasp, know, consider, investigate, or think thoughts [concerning] Him, blessed be He. However we can grasp a little of the mystery [or: principle][24] of His awesome *ways* which are His awesome attributes *(middot)* in so far as He created all the worlds with them. (Shekel HaKodesh p.6)

God Himself is beyond thought and cannot be known or comprehended. But, in so far as He created the visible universe, it is possible to come to know his *ways*, which are the moral attributes *(middot)* by which He governs His world. Moses de Leon expands upon these familiar Maimonidean themes in another work, and in so doing places the main doctrines of kabbalistic theology firmly within the Maimonidean tradition:

> Know that the Creator, blessed be He, is a unified One with no additional composition; that He is the cause of all the causes in that He is the One which has no second nor any limitation. [He is the cause] in that He is recognized in the mystery [or: principle] of his revealed actions and that all of the worlds are dependent on the mystery [or: principle] of His being. For He supports them and they all exist through His power, since He causes them to exist through His mystery [or: principle] and His skill. Indeed the mystery [or: principle] of all the worlds exists through the existence of the *ten sephirot* which are themselves dependent upon that which has no essence *(blimah)*. For everything exists in a hierarchy [or: levels], one above the other, one lofty being above another, as he said: "One high being watches over another, with even higher beings above them." (Eccl. 5:7) (Shoshan Eduth p.333)

---

[24]*Sod* – On this difficult term see SLDN note to line 8.

## INTRODUCTION

Just as in Maimonides' description of the universe, here too all of reality is arranged in a hierarchy of interconnected levels which lead back to their unitary source in the Unitary Creator. The entire created world, both physical and spiritual, is dependent on His *ten sephirot*, which, as we will see immediately, are the *middot* through which He governs the universe. In turn these *ten sephirot* are dependent on the One which is above them.

> With regard to the mystery [or: principle] of this matter, you can know [God], in so far as you recognize and know the mystery [or: principle] of the levels which stand one above the other: from this, one can know the level of the Lord, blessed be He. It is thus because the revealed levels exist one above the other, until they ascend to the mystery [or: principle] of the awesome face from which the light emerges.... Therefore you can know that the awesome brilliant and shining face is the *ten sephirot blimah*, and these are they (in that they are the totality of everything which is included in the mystery [or: principle] of His Name, Blessed be He, though in a certain sense He and His Name are One): *Keter Elyon, Hochmah, Bina, Hesed, Gevurah, Tiferet, Netsah, Hod, Yesod, Malchut* – while these are their names, they also have other names in accordance with their actions, for all of the governance of the worlds are governed by their mysteries [or: principles] ... Through them you can know that He, blessed be He, is a unified One, with neither second nor composition, and that He governs the world through the mystery [or: principle] of His Name, blessed be He. (Ibid pp. 333–334)

Here for the first time me meet the familiar names of the *ten sephirot: Keter Elyon, Hochmah, Bina, Hesed, Gevurah, Tiferet, Netsah, Hod, Yesod, Malchut*. We are also told what they are: they are God's Name through which He both created and governs the revealed world. By ascending in knowledge through the revealed levels, one can reach a knowledge of the hidden levels of the *awesome face*, which is His Name. Since It and He are in some sense one, through It one can come to know Him.

On the one hand, this schema is identical to that of Maimonides. There is the objective order of the created universe, rising up through the great chain of being back toward the One from whom it all descends. The One Himself cannot be known. The highest things one can know are the principles of His creation and providence, which are manifest in the actions which proceed from them. The names we apply to these creative and providential forces are derived from the actions which proceed from them.

On the other hand, there is a definite shift, not just in the writing style, or means of expression, but in the very substance of the thought. These attributes are not merely abstractions of the creative and providential power of the Unknown One. They are called His Name, and are in some way co-equally divine with Him. The common theme of this school that "before God created the world He and His Name were one," (Shekel p. 15) represents a departure from Maimonidean metaphysics, and hearkens back to older rabbinic and midrashic themes. For this reason, these Kabbalists tend to show as much concern for the unity of the Name as Maimonides shows for the unity of God Himself, though, here too, the meaning of the term "unity" seems to be substantially different.

### The Circle of the Zohar and Maimonidean Spirituality

The precise metaphysical content and significance of the Divine Name, and its relation to God and the world, are the primary concerns of this work as a whole. But, before entering into such an abstruse and difficult exposition, the doctrine of the Name, i.e. the Ten Sephirot, must be placed into a religious context, so that its internal dynamic and spiritual significance can be brought into focus.

### Dvekut and Individual Providence

Already in Joseph Gikatilia's time this significance had become obscured, and confused minds approached the study of Kabbalah without a clear understanding of the proper attitude they should adopt in its study. As a result, he composed an introduction to his work *Shaare Orah*, whose whole purpose was to clarify the religious context into which the positive doctrines of the Kabbalah should be placed. The fact that *Shaare Orah* has long been acknowledged by both traditional and academic scholars as the best introduction to the Zohar gives this text an added importance and significance.[25] He opens the work with a personal appeal to the reader, reminiscent of Maimonides' opening dedication to his *Guide:*

---

[25]*Major Trends* p.212; *Aroch HaShulchan, Yoreh Deah* 246:15.

## INTRODUCTION

> You asked me, my brother, friend of my soul, to illuminate a path before you concerning the names of the Holy One, blessed be He, to achieve with them your will, and to arrive through them at your desired goal. Since I understood your intention to be more straight and better than your question, I found it necessary to inform you of the way in which light is apportioned, and of the way which the Name, blessed be He, desires or does not desire. When you finally arrive at a knowledge of this matter, then will you call and God will answer, and you will be among those who are close to Him, and you will love Him with all your soul, and take pleasure from God, and He will grant you all your heart's desires. (Shaare Orah p.45)

Gikatilia was concerned that his readers would misconstrue the kabbalistic doctrines concerning God's names as a magical discipline which gives its master direct power over hidden divine forces. The student whom Gikatilia addresses here, has apparently requested initiation into the secrets of the Kabbalah for precisely this purpose. Gikatilia criticizes this request, finding it reprehensible. But He nevertheless decides to encourage the student's underlying desire to learn about the inner hidden worship of God, whose true character he undertakes to explain to him.

In a sense he has summarized his entire introduction in the final sentence of this opening passage. First you attain to the proper knowledge. Then prayer will be answered. This acceptable prayer consists of four things in the following order of importance: 1) you will be close to Him; 2) you will love Him with all your soul; 3) you will derive great spiritual pleasure; 4) your earthly needs will also be answered. The student's error lay in seeking this final point alone, unaware of its necessary connection to the other several stages. He is, in effect, a simple religious man, accustomed to the external sense of prayer as petition for earthly needs. He mistakenly thought that Kabbalah would give him an alternative *means* of attaining this same exoteric goal. Gikatilia wishes to clarify to him that this is not the case. Rather, to enter into the world of Kabbalah means a radical reorientation of ones very values and goals.

> It is both the definition of truth and the tradition of the covenant that whoever wishes to achieve his desired goals concerning the names of the Holy One, blessed be He, should occupy himself with all his strength in the study of Torah in order to comprehend the sense of each and every one of the holy names that are mentioned in the Torah like *'hyh, yh, yhvh, 'dny, 'l, 'lvh, 'lhym,*

> *shdy, tsb'vt.* One should know and understand that all of these names are like keys to each and every thing that man needs for every aspect and matter in the world. And when one contemplates these names, he finds that all of the Torah and the commandments are dependent upon them. (Ibid p.47)

One who wishes to enter into the true inner worship of God, should not turn away from the concrete content of traditional Judaism. He should not contemplate the Ineffable. Rather he should occupy himself wholly with the study of Torah. In studying, the student should not allow himself to be distracted by grammatical or trivial exigetical concerns. Rather, he should concentrate on the essential content of the Torah: God's creative and providential actions, whether they are manifest in nature, history, or commandment. In particular, the student should pay attention to which name of God is used in which context, since the various names refer to different aspects of his creative and providential power.

> And when he knows the sense of each of these names, he will recognize and know the greatness of He who spoke and the world came to be. Then he will tremble before Him and fear Him, and he will ache and long [for Him] and be filled with an overwhelming desire to cleave to Him through a knowledge of His names, blessed be He. (Ibid)

This passage is an obvious paraphrase of Maimonides' formulation of the commandments of love and fear of God cited above. But it is not merely linguistically similar. It is also systemically identical. For Maimonides, one comes to the love and fear of God by contemplating the principles of God's creative and providential power. It is true that one arrives at these principles by abstracting them from the order of the physical universe. But it is not the universe which is the object of love and fascination, but rather God's *middot* which are manifest in its governance. For Gikatilia, one arrives at these principles by abstracting them from the order manifest in the prophetic texts. But he also agrees that the universe is a direct manifestation of these *middot*. Indeed, he would also agree with Maimonides that the prophets themselves attained their knowledge through direct contemplation of reality. But once this knowledge becomes transcribed in prophetic texts, they become the surest guide to the proper understanding of reality and the divine forces which govern it.

> Then he will be close to God and his prayer will be accepted. Concerning this it is written: "I will keep him safe, because he knew My name. When he calls Me, I shall answer him" (Ps. 91:14–15). The verse did not say "I will keep him safe because he mentioned my name," but rather "because he *knew* my name" – *knowledge* is the essential point. Afterwards – "When he calls Me, I shall answer him." That is to say, whenever he needs something and directs his mind to that name upon which that thing depends, then "I shall answer him." (Ibid)

It is knowledge, not emotional mystification or mechanical theurgy, which is the true key to the hidden worship of God. It is only knowledge which can guarantee the earthy well being which comes from true individual providence – even though this is not the primary goal of knowledge, but rather a secondary by-product.[26] This is a clear expansion and development of the Maimonidean notion of individual providence mentioned above. However, instead of general well being assured by a general intellectual link to God's providence as a whole, here a specific intellectual link to a specific aspect of God's providential power results in a specific type of earthly well being.

In summary: Gikatilia has made it clear that the primary religious significance of the doctrine of the divine names, i.e. the *sephirot*, is that through the knowledge of God's creative and providential *middot*, one comes to *cleave* to God in true love and fear of Him. As a secondary result of this intellectual intimacy, one is included in the sphere of God's individual providence.

## Imitatio Dei

As we saw above in our review of Maimonides' position, *dvekut*, cleaving to God, and *hashgacha*, providence are only one side of the doctrine of God's *middot*. It performs another function of perhaps even greater religious significance – it provides the model for the religious obligation of *imitatio dei*, imitation of God. Gikatilia

---

[26]Cf. *Mishneh Torah*, Repentence 10:2.

devotes the second half of his introduction to explaining this side of the doctrine of the *sephirot*. But before he begins, he warns the reader, in true Maimonidean style,[27] against ascribing any anthropomorphic terms directly to God Himself:

> A General Rule: Know that the reality of the Creator's essence, blessed be He, cannot be grasped by anyone other than Himself... If this is so, what then are all of those matters which we read in the Torah, like *hand* and *foot*, *ear* and *eye*, and all similar matters? Know and believe, that all of these matters, even though they indicate and testify to His greatness and His reality, there is no creature that can know or contemplate the essence of that thing which is called *hand*, or *foot*, or *ear*, and so on. (Ibid p.49)

After this warning, he proceeds to explain his understanding of the notion that man is created in God's image:

> And even if we are created in the image and the form [of God], don't think for a moment that [our] eye is in the form of [His] eye literally, or [our] hand is in the form of [His] hand literally. Rather these are inner matters from the innermost matters in the reality of God's existence, blessed be He, from which the source and the flow of being emerge to all existing beings through the decree of the Name, blessed be He. But the essence of [our] hand is not like the essence of [His] hand, nor are their forms the same, as it is written: "To whom shall you liken me that I should be comparable?" Know and believe that there is no similarity between us and Him with regard to essence or form. (Ibid)

Even though God, strictly speaking, has no form or image in the ordinary sense, it is nevertheless true that we are created in IIis image. How is this so? God's *middot* are the root and source of all of God's creation, including the concrete form of man. Man, who is grasped in both the Jewish philosophical and the kabbalistic traditions as a *microcosm*, is a manifestation of the totality of God's *middot*. Therefore, each of our limbs is in some sense a manifestation of an aspect of God's *middot*. That aspect which is the source of our hand is called His hand. That aspect which is the source of our eye is called His eye.

> Rather the meaning of the form of our limbs lies in their having been made as a kind of signs, matters both high and obscure which the mind cannot

---

[27]Cf. *Mishneh Torah*, Foundations 1:9–10.

know except as a kind of mentioning: as if one were to write *"Reuven the son of Yaacov."* For these letters are not the form, the shape, or the essence of *Reuven the son of Yaacov*, but rather a way of referring to him – such that this written *Reuven the son of Yaacov* is a sign corresponding to the familiar essence and form which is called *Reuven the son of Yaacov*. (Ibid)

Even though there is an ontological link between God's "hand" and our hand, one can in no way derive from the nature of our hand anything substantial about His hand. What then is the meaning of this ontological link?

But since God, blessed be He, wished to ennoble us, He created in the body of man various limbs, both hidden and revealed, which are a kind of sign to the *Work of the Chariot*. And if a man should succeed in purifying one of his limbs, then that limb will be a kind of *throne* for that high inner thing which is called by this name, whether it be an eye, or a hand, or any of the rest. How is this so? For example, if a man should be careful and guard his sight such that he does not look or stare at any forbidden sexual object or any other reprehensible object, but rather only at things which are God's holiness and His worship, then that eye has become like a *throne* to that thing which is called eye above. Similarly with hand and foot, and the rest of all the limbs. (Ibid p.49–50)

While the lower hand may tell us nothing of the upper hand, the upper hand tells us everything about the lower hand. The upper hand is the model for what the lower hand may become. If the lower human form purifies itself, then it becomes an expression on earth of the pure upper divine "human" form, i.e. the *middot* or *sephirot*. In such a case, the lower form becomes a concrete manifestation on earth of God's glory, or in Gikatilia's words, a *throne*. But it is important to remember that it is not the external shape of the limb which is the true image of God. Only when the external *actions* of that limb are in line with the proper internal ethical *middot* does the limb as a whole become a *throne*.

Note: The importance of this doctrine for the theory of kabbalistic symbolism cannot be over emphasized. Each concrete symbol which is applied to God's *middot* represents an act of mapping between two worlds: the lower earthly world in which the concrete image has it existence and the upper divine world which is the ontological root of the lower entity. The concrete entity cannot tell you anything directly about its ontological root. Such knowledge can only be gained through speculative knowledge of God's *middot* themselves. But the symbol as a particular concrete manifestation of the *middot* on earth can focus upon and refer to a particular aspect of the *middot* above. In turn, the meaning of that aspect is to a large extent dependent upon the precise way in which the concrete earthly entity is a manifestation of its divine root. In other words, a kabbalistic symbol represents a complex motion in thought between two distinct semantic fields, each of which must be known prior to the act of of interpreting the symbol. For this reason an adequate analysis of kabbalistic symbolism can only be done *after* a fairly thorough introduction to kabbalistic theology, on the one hand, and to kabbalistic ethics and religious law, on the other.

## The Elements of the Divine Name

### The Divine Name: Knowable and Unknowable

Up to this point, our analysis has shown the extent to which the kabbalistic doctrine of the *sephirot* is continuous with earlier facets of medieval Jewish spirituality. It has focused upon the role which this doctrine plays in the spiritual ideals of love, fear, and imitation of God. Most importantly, it has shown the essentiality of *knowledge* to this entire spiritual program. It is the primary goal of the remainder of this work to expound the fundamental elements of this knowledge, both in the Zohar's words and in our own. But in order to do so, we must first cut ourselves loose from the familiar moorings of medieval Jewish thought which have so far been our guide, and reorient ourselves within the new intellectual and spiritual world which the circle of the Zohar created.

The ten *sephirot* and their familiar names have already been mentioned above. What knowledge can one have of them? Scholem maintained that they are ten equally primitive symbolic expressions of the ineffable divine life, and as such transcend discursive human knowledge.[28] This view would tend to undercut the religious functions of the *sephirot*, which as we have seen are dependent upon positive knowledge. Moreover, the Kabbalists of the circle of the Zohar explicitly reject this notion. Even though they reserve a place for the ineffable in their doctrines, they clearly set out the dividing line between what can be known and what cannot:

First of all you must know that which the Sages said: "'Should you but ask about the first days which were before you, from the day on which God

---

[28]*Major Trends* pp. 208–209 and p. 225.

created man on the earth, and from one end of the heaven to the other.'(Deut. 4:32) [From one end of the heaven to the other] you have permission to speak; from here on: 'That which is too wondrous for you do not seek, and that which is hidden do not investigate; you have no business with hidden things.'" The point is that it is true that the human mind cannot grasp or know that which cannot be defined in thought, nor can it investigate, lest its foundation be ruined and its thought become confused. . . Concerning the statement *From one end of the heaven to the other* . . . they are the mystery of the five sephirot which emerge from *repentence* [Bina] and below . . . From this mystery and above: "No eye has seen it God other than You." (Isa. 64:3) (Ten Sephirot pp.371-374)

Only the first three of the ten *sephirot* are beyond ordinary human investigation. The last seven, which emerge from *Bina*, are open and available for question and answer. This leaves plenty of room for mystical exploration beyond the limits of human knowledge. But it also locates it fairly clearly in the upper three *sephirot*, especially in the first *sephirah*, since, as we shall see in the body of this work, some indirect knowledge is possible of the second and third *sephirot*.[29]

### The Divine Name: Internal Structure

Having made this initial distinction between the upper hidden *sephirot* and the lower ones which are somewhat revealed, we may proceed to ask a series of questions whose goal is to clarify the true nature of these mysterious *sephirot*. The most striking fact concerning these lower seven *sephirot* is that they are not, in the circle of the Zohar, given equal weight. They are not seven or ten primary and equally primitive forces, but rather various aspects or permutations of two primary forces, *Kindness* and *Judgement*, which are identified with God's *right* and *left* hands respectively.

The starting point for our analysis is the following synopsis of the main body of Moses de Leon's *Shekel HaKodesh*, which illustrates quite clearly the internal articulation of the seven lower *sephirot*:

[pp. 36-42] **The Gate of the End of the Heaven:** "Should you but ask about the first days which were before you, from the day on which God

---

[29]See "The Concept of the Divine Name" §13 note 42.

created man on the earth, and from one end of the heaven to the other." You already know and have considered up to what point it is proper for man to ask and to inquire in line with the mystery [or: principle] of the methods of inquiry in order to know something of the reality of His existence, blessed be His name. (p. 36) . . . Consider that the beginning of the matter of His existence . . . which is the End of the Heaven . . . it is the *first light, Grace, Abraham, Right, South, Water,* . . . *Love.* . . (p. 38)

[pp. 42-47] **The Gate of the North:** which is the root of *elemental fire* . . . and it is called *the terror of Isaac, Might, the Attribute of Harsh Judgement.* . . *the color red, Darkness, Left, North* . . . (p. 42)

[pp. 47-55] **The Gate of the East:** which is the root of *Air* . . . it is *East, Air,* . . . *Jacob* . . . *Mercy* . . . (p. 47)

[pp. 55-69] **The Gate of the Final Three:** These are the mystery [or: principle] of the three final blessings [of the daily prayer, the Amidah]. . . Indeed the mystery [or: principle] of these final three is that they correspond to the mystery [or: principle] of the upper Patriarchs. (p. 55)

[pp. 70-98] **The Gate of the West:** the principle of [elemental] earth . . . (Shekel HaKodesh pp. 36-98)

    The titles of the main sections into which the work is divided reflect an internal articulation which is echoed precisely in the body of the *Secrets of the Letters* below.[30] This division reveals an interesting symbolic structure. Four *sephirot* are singled out for special treatment: *sephirot* four, five, six, and ten are each identified with one of the four primary directions (NSEW) and one of the primary elements (air, fire, water, earth). They each get a separate section, while *sephirot* seven, eight, and nine are lumped together. Moreover, among the "big four", the first three have a certain primacy. They are each identified with one of the three Patriarchs, Abraham, Isaac, and Jacob, and are each assigned a primary moral attribute, *love, harsh judgement,* and *mercy* respectively.

    The precise relationship among these various *sephirot*, or *heavens*, can be ascertained from the following passages:

---

[30]It should be clear by now that the circle of the Zohar has no fixed terminology for what are later called consistently *sephirot*. They are sometimes called *middot, heavens, levels,* and so on. For the use of the specific term *sephirot* in the Zohar itself and its meaning there, see SLDN note to line 196.

INTRODUCTION

> **The First Heaven** is the Heaven which is called the Heaven of *South*. It is the mystery [or: principle] of *Right* . . . for this Heaven is the element of *Water*. (Shekel haKodesh p. 9)
> **The Second Heaven** is is the Heaven of *North*. It is the *Left* Side, the Elemental *Fire*. (Ibid p. 11)
> **The Third Heaven** is the Heaven which is called the Heaven of *East*. It is the elemental of *Air*. It arbitrates between *Fire and Water*, and they are included in it. (Ibid p. 12)

The first of the seven heavens is *Right*. The second is *Left*. The third is a synthetic force which arbitrates between these two and includes both of them.

> The mystery [or: principle] of the final three [blessings] which are the Three Heavens which are below [these first three]:
> The First Heaven which is the **Fourth Heaven** . . . it is called *Netsah* . . . the mystery [or: principle] of Netsah is the attribute of *Left*. (Ibid p.13)
> The Second Heaven which is the **Fifth Heaven** is called *Hod* and it is the attribute of *Right*. (Ibid p.14)

The following two heavens are characterized only as a repetition of the familiar *middot Left* and *Right*.

> [The **Sixth Heaven**] is the **Heaven** [Rakia'] **of the Sky** [Shamayim] . . . for it takes all the heavenly bodies [ma'orot] and is the totality of them all. For this reason it is called *All*. (Ibid)
> The [Seventh] **Heaven** which is below all the other Heavens . . . is the *Heaven which does nothing* (Hagigah 12b) for the *Moon* [the seventh heaven] has no light of its own at all, only what it receives from the Sun [the sixth which has the heavenly bodies which give light]. (Ibid p.15)

The sixth is the totality of the five previous *middot* in so far as they give light, the seventh is the totality of the five previous *middot* in so far as it receives light. As such, they represent permutations of the same two elements, *left* and *right*.

The Substance of the Divine Name

What is this common denominator of *left* and *right* which runs through all of the seven lower *sephirot?* The following passage provides the key:

Abraham corresponds to the *Right*, for he is the *Attribute of Kindness*. Isaac ... is the *Left* for he is the *Attribute of Harsh Judgement* ... Whereas Jacob is the *Middle Path* which adjudicates between them, for he is the *Attribute of Truth* – and there is only *Truth* when two contrary statements contradict each other, and by struggling with the contradiction the *Truth* finally comes to light. (Shoshan Eduth p. 334)

The *Left* and the *Right* are the two polar extremes of pure wrathful *Judgement* on the one hand and pure forgiving *Kindness (or Compassion)* on the other. The middle path of *Truth,* which is identified with both *Mercy* and *Justice*,[31] is the synthesis which results from the struggle between the two. Even though this dialectic of the *middot* bears a formal similarity to the extremes and the middle path of Maimonidean ethics, and may in fact be intentionally formulated in imitation of this model,[32] the actual content is very far removed from Maimonides' notion of the divine attributes, as we already mentioned above. The source for this dialectic is not however to be found in some heretical underground stream, but in the classical source of orthodox rabbinic monotheism, the Babylonian Talmud.

### The Divine Name and Rabbinic Theology

The elements of rabbinic theology which were incorporated into the doctrine of the Divine Name will be presented systematically below in the body of the work. For the present, we only wish to acquaint the reader with these three aspects of God's *middot*, the two polar extremes of pure wrathful *Judgement*, pure forgiving *Kindness (or Compassion)*, and the middle path of *Mercy*, as they occur in a well known rabbinic text. All of the following passages are taken from the Babylonian Talmud, Tractate *Berachot* 7a:

> Rabbi Yochanon said in the name of Rabbi Yose: From whence do we derive that God prays? From that which is written, "And I will bring them to My holy mountain and make them rejoice in the house of My prayer" (Isa. 56:7) –

---

[31]For the precise difference between *Kindness* and *Mercy* and the relation of *Mercy* to *Justice* see *Shekel HaKodesh* pp.53–55.

[32]Cf. *Shaare Tsedek* 23a, especially the use of Maimonidean terms for the extremes and the middle.

it does not say *their prayer*, but rather *My prayer*. From here we derive that God prays. What is the content of His prayer? Rav Zutra bar Tuvia said in the name of Rav: "May it be acceptable before Me that My Mercies should suppress My Anger, that My Mercies should prevail over My Attributes [of Judgement], so that I behave toward My children with the Attribute of Mercy and be lenient with them [literally: act within the strict line of Judgement]."

This opening passage acquaints us with God's two primary attributes: His *Mercy* and His *Anger* (otherwise known as *Judgement*). It also informs us that the content of God's prayer[33] is that His *Mercies* should restrain His *Anger*. But why should God's *Anger* need to be restrained? What would be so terrible if God were to judge His children "fairly" without any special leniency? These points are clarified in the following passage:

And Rabbi Yochanon said in the name of Rabbi Yose: From whence do we derive that one should not attempt to appease anyone during the moment of his anger? From that which is written, "My Face will go and I will concede to you." (Ex. 33:14) The Holy One, blessed be He, said to Moses: "Wait until My Face of Anger passes, and then I will concede to you." Is there indeed Anger before the Holy One, blessed be He?! Yes, as we have learned [in the following tradition]: "And God is angry every day." (Ps. 7:12) How much is His Anger? A moment. How much is a moment? One part in fifty eight thousand, eight hundred and eighty eight of an hour – this is a moment. And the only creature who was able to find that moment was the evil Balaam, as it is written, "Who knows the knowledge of the Most High" (Num. 24:16) – If he did not even know what his animal knew (cf. Num. 22:22 ff.), how could he know the knowledge of the Most High? Therefore it must mean that he was able to find [and exploit] that moment in which God is angry ... Rabbi Elazar said: The Holy One, blessed be He, said to Israel, "You should know what favors I did for you by not being angry in the days of the evil Balaam, for if I had angered not the slightest remnant of Israel would be left."

God's *Anger*, if released upon the Jewish people, would have destroyed them down to the last man, without distinguishing between the righteous and the wicked.[34] God's *Anger* is the very source of the demonic power of that most evil of all idolatrous

---

[33]For this remarkable image of God praying see Rabbi Azriel of Gerona, *Commentary on the Talmudic Aggadoth*, ed. Tishbi, 2nd edition (Jerusalem 1983) pp. 8-9.

[34]See "The Concept of the Divine Name" §§4-5.

sorcerors, Balaam himself. It is therefore quite clear why God wishes that this pure destructive wrath, which borders on evil itself, should be restrained.

If this is the nature of God's *Anger*, what is the nature of His *Mercy?*

> And Rabbi Yochanon said in the name of Rabbi Yose: Moses requested three things from the Holy One, blessed be He, and He granted him [all three]. He requested that the Shechinah should dwell with Israel . . . He requested that the Shechinah should not dwell with the idolators . . . and he requested that the Holy One, blessed be He, should let him know His *ways* . . . He said before Him: "Master of the Universe, why do some of the righteous prosper while others suffer, why do some of the wicked prosper while others suffer?" . . . This is what He said to him: The righteous who prosper are wholly righteous while the righteous who suffer are not wholly righteous; the wicked who prosper are not wholly wicked, while the wicked who suffer are wholly wicked. This tradition disagrees with the opinion of Rabbi Meir, for Rabbi Meir said: Two requests he was granted, but the third he was denied, as it is written, "And I will have compassion upon those whom I will have compassion and mercy upon those whom I will have mercy" – even if he is not worthy.

The first opinion in this passage holds that all of God's ways are just and equitable. Both the suffering of the righteous and the prosperity of the wicked are only apparently exceptions to the rule of God's justice. But the opinion of Rabbi Meir is quite different. Rabbi Meir holds that the prosperity of the wicked is to be understood as an expression of the inscrutable *Mercy* of the Creator. God's *Mercy* and *Compassion* were not capable of being understood even by Moses himself.

Maimonides' claim that Moses understood all of God's ways may reflect the first position here. In any case, the Zohar explicitly accepted Rabbi Meir's position.[35] According to this position, God's *Mercies* can be granted equally to the righteous and the wicked alike: "And I will have compassion upon those whom I will have compassion and mercy upon those whom I will have mercy" – *even if he is not worthy.*

---

[35] See SLDN ll. 32–42.

## INTRODUCTION

In this regard, His *Mercy* is exactly parallel to His *Anger*. Neither is a rational principle which is meted out to those who deserve them, but rather they are like two antithetical primordial forces, with nothing whatsoever in common. It is therefore no surprise to discover that the Gnostics of the early rabbinic period felt it necessary to ascribe these two contradictory *middot* to two different deities.[36] Fair Judgement, or Justice, only emerges when God's *Mercy* restrains His *Anger*. Neither of the *middot* alone is sufficient. Since this was the content of God's prayer at the beginning of the passage, it would seem that Rabbi Meir's position is in line with the general thrust of this passage as a whole.

### Summary

It is clear that the three kabbalistic *root-middot* of *Kindness*, *Judgement*, and *Mercy* correspond to these two poles of pure *Mercy*, pure *Anger*, and measured *Justice* which results from the struggle between them. In turn, each of the *ten sephirot* is understood as reflecting this triad in one way or another. The first three are their hidden roots. The next three are identified with them. The following three are a reflection of the immediately preceding three. The tenth is understood as the receptacle in which their light is received and then reflected into the lower worlds.

The concern with comprehending the dialectical unity which is supposed to exist between these three *middot* is no idle speculative game. If God's *middot* cannot combine to form a coherent and harmonious whole, directing the dynamic conflict which exists between the extremes in a positive and creative direction, then the human life which is to be modeled on these *middot* will be equally confused and incoherent. Moreover, if this unity and harmony is of a mystical nature, and so beyond human understanding, then it cannot form a basis either for *dvekut* or for *imitatio dei*, the two primary religious concerns of this kabbalistic circle.

It is for this reason that Gikatilia states in no uncertain terms that:

---

[36]See "The Concept of the Divine Name" §1ff.

## THE ELEMENTS OF THE DIVINE NAME

> One should not consider for a moment that these matters which I am telling you now about this root principle are matters which one should accept and believe, but they have no explanation. Rather, these matters are a received tradition, but we have *knowledge* of them, and we are able to give an *explanation* and a *proof* for each of them with respect to our pure Torah, with a kind of *demonstration* visible to the eye. (Shaare Orah pp.186–187)

These references to *explanation, knowledge, proof,* and *demonstration,* come from Gikatilia's introduction to his paraphrase of those doctrines which are contained in the Zohar text *The Secrets of the Letters of the Divine Name.* He may in fact have had this very text in mind, for it is only in *the Secrets of the Letters* that the dialectic of the *middot* is worked out in the kind of detail which could be called anything like a conceptual *proof* or a *demonstration.*

In any case, it should be clear from this that the accepted interpretation of the classical Kabbalah as "essentially an attempt to preserve the substance of naive popular faith, now challenged by the rational theology of the philosophers,"[37] is at best a gross oversimplification, and at worst a misrepresentation of the most basic elements of kabbalistic faith. If anything, the classical Kabbalah could be described as an attempt to return to the substance of traditional rabbinic theology within the spiritualist religious framework of medieval Jewish thought. But the frequently murky depths of classical rabbinic theology are anything but naive and popular, and when developed within the conceptual and spiritual frameworks available to the medieval Jewish sage, the results are quite strikingly profound, original, and compelling.

---

[37] *Major Trends* p.206.

# THE DOCTRINE OF THE DIVINE NAME

## Part One:

## THE CONCEPT OF THE DIVINE NAME

## THE CONCEPT OF THE DIVINE NAME

The first half of *the Secrets of the Letters* is a systematic exposition of a single idea: the concept of the Divine Name, *YHVH*. This concept is built on the foundations of classical rabbinic thought, and draws on the conceptual categories of medieval philosophy. At the same time, the synthetic vision which emerges from this concept transcends the fragmentary elements out of which it grew. The Zohar, as the first mature and fully developed expression of this concept, marks a new beginning in the history of Jewish thought: the start of the mainstream kabbalistic tradition. This tradition claims the immense Zoharic literature as its canonical basis, and the writings of Isaac Luria as its culminating authoritative interpretation. It formed the theological foundation of much of medieval Judaism for more than half a millennium. Echoes of this tradition may still be heard today.

With *the Secrets of the Letters* we return to the very beginnings of this tradition. The purpose of this preliminary exposition is to place the Zohar's highly symbolic conception of the Divine Name in the context of the traditions out of which it grew, to present in outline the synthetic ideas which the Zohar builds out of these elements, and finally to clarify the way in which his[1] symbolic language expresses these ideas. This exposition should provide the reader with a broad overview of the issues, concepts, and symbols contained in *the Secrets of the Letters*. In so doing, it should also allow for a more fruitful initial reading of this very difficult and obscure text.

This exposition also serves a second purpose: it brings together, in a centralized form, all of the various textual and conceptual materials which serve as the *premises* for the commentary to the text. By avoiding unnecessary duplications and digressions, it should facilitate a more straightforward and focused analysis of the text.

The preliminary exposition, which is divided into four main parts, has been subdivided into numbered sections in order to permit easy reference in the commentary.

---

[1] I refer to the anonymous author of the Zohar in the singular as a matter of convenience. I do not intend by this to prejudice the question of the single or multiple authorship of the work. Cf. pp.4–5 above.

## Rabbinic Background

### §1: The Challenge of Dualism

In classical rabbinic literature, the two primary Names of God, *YHVH* and *Elohim*, are identified with the two primary expressions of His providential power: The Attribute of Mercy *(=YHVH)* and the Attribute of Judgement *(=Elohim)*. The Zohar accepts these two fundamental identifications as the foundation of his theology. In this way his understanding of the essential nature of God is rooted in the theological problematics of the rabbinic period.[2]

This doctrine of attributes appears to posit a multiplicity within God. Sectarians, expounding the doctrine of dualism, siezed upon this distinction of different forces within God, and asserted that these two attributes were in fact two separate deities: a higher God of mercy and a lower wrathful Demiurge.[3] Both this heresy and the rabbinic response to it, as recorded in rabbinic literature, take on added significance when discussing the roots of Kabbalistic thought – for it is against the background of the challenge of dualism that the Kabbalistic affirmation of Divine Unity receives its meaning.[4]

On the face of it, it is not at all clear what the dispute between the Rabbis and their dualistic heretics was about. The following text is usually cited as the classic expression of the challenge which dualism posed to rabbinic Judaism:

> "YHVH is a Man of War, YHVH is His Name." (Ex.15.3) Why was this [verse] stated? – because He was revealed to them at the Red Sea as a mighty warrior doing battle ... whereas at Mount Sinai He was revealed to them as an old man, full of mercy ... ; [therefore, the verse was stated] so as not to

---

[2] For a general discussion of these attributes in rabbinic literature see E. E. Urbach, *Hazal* (Jerusalem 1975) p.399ff.

[3] See S. Lieberman, *Tosephta Ki-Fshuta* Part V (New York 1962) pp. 1292–1294.

[4] Despite the centrality of the doctrine of Divine Unity in the theology of the Zohar, it has been asserted that the Zohar's repeated assertions in this regard should not be taken seriously (*Major Trends* p.224). If Scholem had placed the Zohar's notion of Unity in its proper rabbinic context (instead of interpreting it as an Aristotelian philosophical concept), he would not have arrived at such an implausible conclusion. For an unequivocal affirmation of the primacy of speculative understanding of Divine Unity in the Zohar's theology and its specific content, see SLDN 1.564 ff.

give the Nations an excuse to claim that there are Two Powers. (MRI pp.129-130)

It hardly seems a controversial theological point, given the simple sense of the Biblical text, that God punishes his enemies and bestows goodness and mercy upon his friends. Even if one chooses to call the former manifestation of God's power *the Attribute of Judgement*, and the latter *the Attribute of Mercy*, this still does not seem to provide sufficient cause for us to doubt that the same God who saved the Israelites at the Red Sea also gave them the Torah at Sinai.

The text is clearly assuming more about these Divine Attributes than it is stating explicitly. From the following text it is possible to learn something of the theological assumptions which underlie and motivate the dualistic challenge to the rabbinic faith in One God:

> A human warrior, when enveloped by battle fever, may strike down even his own father, mother, or other close relative. However, *He who spoke and the world came to be* is not like this. Rather, "YHVH is a Man of War, YHVH is His Name." *YHVH is a Man of War* in that He fights against the Egyptians. *YHVH is His Name* in that He has mercy upon His creatures, as it is written, "YHVH YHVH, merciful and gracious." (Ex.34.6) (MRI p.130)

Like the first text cited above, this text also discusses the punishment of the Egyptians at the Red Sea. Similarly, it discusses God's Attributes of Judgement and Mercy. But it differs from the previous text in that it attempts to understand the individual roles which each of these attributes played in the punishment of the Egyptians at the Red Sea.

The human warrior described by the text becomes so possessed by battle fever, that he is unable to restrain his fury. He strikes down in his wrath whoever may cross his path, friend and foe alike. The midrash then seeks to distinguish the Divine warrior from this human warrior. The Divine warrior does not strike down friend and foe alike, for He is not carried away by His wrath, but rather rules over it and restrains it.

This theme is expanded upon by the following related midrash:

> For I, *YHVH*, your God *(Elohim)*, am a God of Wrath (Ex.20.5): For I am the God of Wrath – I rule over wrath, and wrath does not rule over me.[5] (MRI p.226)

In our text also, God is portrayed as the Master of His wrath. At the same time that God was striking down the Egyptians, He was also restraining His wrath, directing it against those who deserved to be destroyed, while saving the Israelites.

### §2: Mercy and Judgement as Logically Incompatible

The midrash ascribes to the Attribute of Judgement *the battle against the Egyptians*. To the Attribute of Mercy it ascribes God's *mercy upon His creatures*. If we have understood correctly that the function of Mercy here is to restrain wrath, then the implication would be that God's wrath, if unrestrained, would strike down friend and foe alike, just like human wrath. On the other hand, if *restraint* is the only function of the Attribute of Mercy here, and the actual war against the Egyptians is being carried out by the Attribute of Judgement, it would seem that the Attribute of Mercy, if left to itself, would punish no one, not even the wicked who deserve punishment.

This interpretation of God's Attributes finds some confirmation in a rabbinic parable concerning the roles that the Attributes played in the creation of the world. Commenting on the verse, "When *YHVH-Elohim* made heaven and earth" (Gen. 2.4), the midrash offers the following parable:

> *YHVH-Elohim:* This is comparable to a King who had empty glasses. The King said: "If I put hot water in them, they will burst. [If I put] cold water in them, they will crack. What did the King do? He mixed hot and cold water together, put it in them, and they did not break. Thus spoke the Holy One, blessed be He: If I create the world with the Attribute of Mercy, then the sinners will become numerous. [If I create it] with the Attribute of Judgement, the world will be unable to stand. So, I will create it with [both] the Attribute of Judgement and the Attribute of Mercy – Oh that it would stand! – *YHVH-Elohim*. (BR pp.112–113)

---

[5]I have translated *kin'ah* in this passage as wrath (not as *jealousy*) in order to bring out more clearly the text's primary concern: the violent consequences of God's emotional response to provocation. Cf. §5 below.

The Attribute of Mercy *(YHVH)* and the Attribute of Judgement *(Elohim)* are compared to *hot* and *cold*, two polar opposites, either of which, if left to itself, would destroy the world. Only by mixing them together, so that the heat of the one mitigates the cold of the other, and vice versa, can the world be expected to stand. If the world were created with the attribute of Mercy alone, the wicked would multiply. Why? Because Mercy will not punish anyone, even those who deserve punishment. If the world were created with Judgement alone, all would be destroyed, for there would be no Mercy to limit the destructive force of Judgement to those who truly deserve it.[6]

In these sources, the Rabbis understand the Divine Attributes as antithetical polar opposites, like the extremes of hot and cold – *pure destructive wrath* and *pure, absolutely forgiving mercy*. If this is the case, then the problem of ascribing them both to a single God is not that of ascribing *multiple* attributes to a single subject, but rather that of ascribing *contradictory* attributes to a single subject.

### §3: Mercy and Judgement as Morally Incompatible

According to this understanding of rabbinic thought, the punishment of the wicked can be effected only through the agency of the Attribute of Judgement – a wrathful principle, whose nature, unrestrained by Mercy, borders on evil itself. If God does not punish the wicked, however, what then can one make of the Law, with its promises of reward and punishment in this world and the next? If one wishes to keep the concept of the merciful God pure and unsullied by the dark side of wrath, then it might be necessary to give up not only the notions of Divine Justice and the Law, but also any other positive interest in this unfortunate and evil world, whose continued existence is predicated on the governance of this evil principle. This

---

[6]By "truly deserve it" is meant: in accordance with those lenient standards of Judgement which incorporate the rabbinic notions of *measure for measure* and *teshuvah*. See Urbach op. cit. pp. 384–392, 408–415. For more strict categories of Judgement see below §§4 and 5, and Zohar vol. 3 231.

is the logic of the dualist position, and there were not a few proponents of this position who drew these very conclusions.[7]

For the Rabbis, who were commited both to the value of Justice and *to the religious significance of life in this world*, this path offered no solution. The ideal of a merciful God would have to be maintained alongside the notion of Divine wrath. In so far as wrath was needed to exact punishment from the wicked, they included it in their concept of God. In so far as wrath would extend beyond its legitimate bounds and cruelly afflict the innocent, they attempted to exclude it from their concept of God as much as possible.

The tensions between these theological assumptions and commitments involved the tradition of rabbinic thought in a dangerous balancing act between two extremes, either of which spelled disaster for their ethical and spiritual ideals. The texts cited in the following two sections do not provide any solution to this dilemma. They merely illustrate the depth of the problem, and the seriousness with which the rabbinic tradition took it.

### §4: The Destroyer

When informing the Israelites in Egypt of His intention to strike down the first born of the Egyptians, God warns them that "no one should go outside of his house until morning." (Ex.12.22) From this warning, the midrash draws the following conclusion:

> This teaches that once permission is given to the Destroyer to strike, he does not distinguish between the righteous and the wicked.[8] (MRI p.38)

The fact that God felt it necessary to warn the Israelites to stay indoors implies that if an Israelite were to venture outside his house while the Destroyer was striking down the Egyptians, he too would be struck down – irrespective of his own personal innocence and righteousness. So long as the righteous Israelite remains indoors, he will be protected from the destructive wrath of the Destroyer – but

---

[7]See Hans Jonas, *The Gnostic Religion*, 2nd ed. Boston 1963, esp. pp. 42–47; also A. Harnack, *Marcion. Das Evangelium vom fremden Gott*, 2nd ed. Leipzig 1924, and A. Marmorstein, "The Background of the Haggadah," *HUCA* vol 6 (1929) pp. 141–204.

[8]Cf. SLDN ll.93–101

only by the blood of the Passover lamb placed upon the doorposts of his house, not by his righteousness.

This Destroyer fits the description of unrestrained wrath precisely. Yet it is not portrayed as a direct expression of God's providential power. Rather God *gives it permission to strike*, and God *prevents it from entering* the houses of the Israelites. While legitimate expression of wrath is ascribed directly to God (*YHVH* is a Man of War), illegitimate wrath which strikes down the innocent is ascribed to the absence of God:

> "And YHVH will protect the door and He will not let [the Destroyer enter]" (Ex.12.23) – If concerning the blood of the Passover sacrifice in Egypt, which is a minor commandment ... it says "He will not let the Destroyer enter", then it certainly follows that [if we fulfill] the commandment of the Mezuzah, which is a more important commandment ... He should not let the Destroyer enter [our houses.] What then has caused [this to occur]? Our sins, as it is written, "But your iniquities have been a barrier between you and your God; your sins have made Him turn His face away and refuse to hear you." (Is.59.2) (MRI p.39)

This midrash does not attempt to justify the harsh judgements of the Destroyer. The very concept of the Destroyer is *indifference to righteousness and wickedness,* and so its judgements are inherently evil. The question which the author asks is: Why have God's mercies not protected us from the evil Destroyer as they did in Egypt? To this he answers: Our communal sins have separated between us and God, causing God's mercies to withdraw, and so exposing the righteous to cruel punishments which only the wicked deserve.

§5: The Cruelty of the Merciful One

The Zohar is fairly consistent in differentiating between the legitimate judgement which may be ascribed directly to God, and the cruel, harsh judgement which must be excluded from the unity of the Divine Name. Rabbinic texts are not always so careful, and in this regard may be considered more radical than the Kabbalah of the Zohar.[9]

---

[9]But see SLDN ll. 230-231 and notes to lines 222-223.

We already saw above that the phrase *God of wrath* was understood as reflecting God's domination and restraint of His wrath. Another interpretation of the same verse is not so sure of this point:

> "For I, YHVH your God, am a God of wrath." With wrath I exact punishment for Idolatry, but I am merciful in other matters. (MRI p.226)

Here *a God of wrath* is understood in its simple sense: *a wrathful God*. Moreover His wrath is opposed to His mercy, implying that when He is wrathful, He is *not* merciful. The one concession to the notion of *YHVH* as an essentially merciful God, is the limitation of wrath to the most extreme of all crimes.

The notion that God sometimes judges with wrath unrestrained by Mercy is implicit in this text. In the following text this notion is mentioned explicitly:

> When the Nations heard that the Holy One, blessed be He, was championing the cause of Israel ... they became angry. The Holy One, blessed be He, said to them, "Fools that you are! How many of your kings ruled and Israel did not become angry? ... and now you are becoming angry?! So also *I will give you anger without compassion!*" (MRI p.146)

But only in the following text do notions like God's anger and cruelty play a central role in a general rule of His providence:

> When Israel does God's will, there is no anger before Him ... but when they do not do God's will, there is anger before Him ... When Israel does God's will, He fights for them ... but when they do not do God's will, he fights against them ... and, moreover, *they make the Merciful cruel.* (MRI p.137)

### §6: The Legacy of Rabbinic Judaism

Scholem doubted whether the Zohar's "mythical heritage has everywhere been successfully integrated into the doctrine of monotheism."[10] While I agree substantially with Professor Scholem's characterization of the problematic character of the Zohar's thought, it is important to remember that kabbalistic theology developed not only as a response to its immediate predecessors (most notably

---

[10] *Major Trends* p.225

Maimonides), but also as a continuation of older, far more authoritative traditions. The preceding sections have shown that the classical rabbinic tradition itself contains many of the very elements which Scholem considered incompatable with monotheism: the notion of a multiplicity of forces within God, bordering on dualism; the insistence upon finding the unity within this multiplicity, even at the risk of including the roots of evil within God himself. Some of these elements may not be reconcilable with the monotheism of thinkers like Maimonides. But these thinkers, despite their importance, cannot, by themselves, be taken as the sole standard by which either to judge or to understand the Zohar.[11]

The problems of rabbinic and kabbalistic theology do not stem from an inability to bend their principles into line with some external standard. Rather their problems are internal – their difficulties arise *immanently* out of the complex of assumptions and commitments which form the basis of their understanding of God and His Will concerning man. The Zohar's theological task is to transcend the contradictions which threaten rabbinic Judaism, without compromising the fundamental assumptions and commitments which gave rise to them.

**Philosophical Elements**

§7: Love and Strife in Kabbalistic Theology

If one were to view the rabbinic concepts Mercy and Judgement abstractly, one could define them as positive and negative moral forces, which play some role in the creation of the world. But when the Zohar comes to elaborate upon the creative role of Judgement and Mercy, it becomes apparent that he is not merely abstracting from the rabbinic tradition, but also supplementing it with conceptual categories which are drawn, directly or indirectly, from the medieval traditions ascribed to the Greek philosopher Empedocles.[12]

---

[11]Cf. *Major Trends* p.38

[12]The origins and unusual prominence of Empedoclean and Pseudo-Empedoclean influences on the development of philosophy in Moslem Spain remain somewhat of a mystery. See C. Brockelman, *History of the Islamic Peoples* (London 1948) p.190, and

According to the authentic opinions of the Greek Philosopher Empedocles, there are two primary moving forces in reality: Love and Strife. "All things unite in one through Love."[13] Strife, on the other hand, is the cause of separation, opposition and antagonism. These cosmic forces, which play a dominant role in the ordering of the physical universe, run through *all* of reality, including the ethical human sphere. Scholars believe Empedocles to have held that "sexual love and cosmic Love are one and the same self-existent external force which acts upon the person or the thing that loves."[14] Aristotle also gave Empedocles' concepts Love and Strife a fundamentally moral interpretation:

> For if we were to follow out the view of Empedocles, and interpret it according to its meaning and not to its lisping expression, we should find that Love is the cause of good things, and Strife of bad. Therefore, if we said that Empedocles in a sense both mentions, and is the first to mention, the bad and the good as principles, we should perhaps be right.[15]

The Zohar's doctrine of Divine Attributes displays this same fusion of moral and conceptual principles.[16] In it, too, an understanding of the Divine nature is constructed out of intuitions concerning the nature of human sexual love.[17] It does not matter whether the author of the Zohar was personally acquainted with the Neo-Platonic literature available in his time.[18] The important point is that he had access to logical and ontological concepts which fit his

---

Majid Fakhry, *A History of Islamic Philosophy*, 2nd edition (New York 1983) pp.257–259.

[13] G. S. Kirk and J. E. Raven, *The Presocratic Philosophers*, (Cambridge University Press, London and New York 1971) p.327

[14] Ibid p.330

[15] Ibid

[16] In the Zohar's presentation of the Work of Creation (vol. 1 17a–18a), Judgement functions as a principle of separation and opposition (*mahloqet* = strife or dissention) which gives rise to antagonism between the elements of creation; Mercy, on the other hand, functions as a principle of harmony or peace which unifies these conflicting elements together as one. In an early text (ZHM21b), the Zohar calls this primordial force of unity "the Love (*havivuta*) which is before the Holy One, blessed be He."

[17] See §11 below and end of §12.

[18] Cf. *Major Trends* p.203

theological tradition well, and which could help him sort out the complexities of the tradition which he had inherited.

### §8: Love and Strife as Formal Causes

Medieval Jewish thinkers, like the Zohar, probably had access to some of Empedocles' authentic opinions. But it was primarily through the syncretic medium of the medieval Neo-Platonic tradition that his ideas were known and had their influence.[19] The two main categories of his philosophy, Love and Strife, were integrated into this tradition as the *formal causes* of spirituality and corporeality:

> Matter, according to its essence, is composed of Love and Strife. From these two [principles] the *simple, spiritual substances*, and the *composite, corporeal substances* were made – in such a way that Love and Strife may be considered two attributes or two forms for the substance, two principles for the totality of existing beings. Spiritual things receive in their fullness the imprint of Pure Love, while corporeal things receive in their fullness the imprint of Strife; the things which are composed of both receive both impressions, Love and Strife, Empathy and Enmity.[20]

The specific notion that corporeality derives from Strife is directly incorporated in one of the Zohar's more important presentations of the Work of Creation.[21] But since the Zohar's authoritative midrashic sources already contained a theory concerning the origins of the physical world and the spiritual world, the integration of the overall doctrine contained in this passage takes an interesting turn:

> "For with *YH*, *YHVH* created worlds." (Is.28.4) These are the Two Worlds which the Holy One, blessed be He, created – one with *H* and one with *Y*. I would not know whether the World to Come [was created] with *Y* and This World with *H*, or This World [was created] with *Y* and the World to Come with *H*. But when [the Torah] says: "This is the story of the heavens and the earth when they were created," (Gen.2.4) – don't read it as *when they were*

---

[19]See Jacques Schlanger, *The Philosophy of Solomon Ibn Gabirol* (Jerusalem 1979) p.71.

[20]Ibid p.73

[21]Cf. Zohar vol. 1 18a: the existence (*qiyuma*) and the inhabitation (*yishuva*) of the world are ascribed to Strife (*mahloqet*).

*created*, but rather as *with H He created them:* that is to say that This world [was created] with *H* and the World to Come with *Y*.[22]

The Zohar combines these two traditions by a simple equation. The Zohar's conceptual model tells him that the spiritual world derives from the principle of Mercy (Love) and the physical world from the principle of Judgement (Strife). His midrashic source, on the other hand, ascribes This World (the physical world) to the first letter *yod*, and the World to Come (the spiritual world)[23] to the second letter *he* of the Divine Name. So it follows: the first letter *yod* = the principle of Mercy (Love), and the second letter *he* = the principle of Judgement (Strife).

### §9: Love and Strife as Logical Principles

In addition to these physical, moral, and formal functions, Love and Strife also play a role in the realm of pure thought – as the logical principles of identity and difference. Medieval sources ascribed the following doctrine to Empedocles:

> He [Empedocles] says: This [i.e. the imprint of Love and Strife] is the meaning of the homogeneous being unified (whether individuals, species, or genera), and of the heterogeneous being separate, such that individuals repel each other, species repel each other, genera repel each other.[24]

According to this doctrine, both the specificity of essential definitions (species and genera), and the identity of individuals, derive from Strife, the force of opposition. Similarly, the unification of distinct individuals under the heading of a single species, or of different species under the heading of a single genus, or even the

---

[22] Babylonian Talmud Menachot 29b, Palestinian Talmud Hagigah 77c, Pesikta Rabbati 21, Genesis Rabbah 12.10, Midrash Psalms 62.1. This source plays a major role in the Zohar literature – see Reuven Margaliot, *Shaare Zohar* (Jerusalem 1978) p.117 b–c.

[23] The clear identification the World to Come with spiritual reality (as opposed to the Resurrection of the Dead) was made already by Maimonides in *Mishneh Torah*, Repentence cp. 8. See also Urbach op. cit. pp.587–589.

[24] Schlanger op. cit. p.73

unity of the various limbs within an individual, all reflect the unifying force of Love.

This notion, which plays a role in the later development of European philosophy,[25] asserts that specific finite form is possible only through negation and opposition. Black is only recognizable as a distinct notion through its opposition to white.[26] Without this element of opposition, there would be no specific colors, only color in general. Without the opposition of sight to taste, there would be no specific senses, only sensation in general. Remove the notions of opposition and negation totally, and all concepts would collapse into a single all encompassing notion, like Being, in which everything (and nothing) is included.

Similarly, without the element of unity, which overcomes differences, all genera would break up into species, all species into individuals, all individuals into an infinity of divisible parts until no intelligible form remained.

It is important to point out that Love and Strife, in their roles as logical principles, are not restricted to epistemology, to the *cognition* of reality, but are rather themselves the ontological categories which *constitute* reality itself. If there were no principle of negation, it is not merely the subjective concepts of black and white, good and bad, righteous and wicked, that would collapse – the realities to which these concepts refer would themselves *cease to be*.

Following this line of reasoning, the Zohar describes the extremes of both Mercy and of Judgement as *formless*. In the upper reaches of Mercy the light is so brilliant that there is no "white or black or red or green – there is no color at all." Since no discernible form

---

[25]Hegel based his own version of this notion (*Die Bestimmtheit ist die Negation als affirmativ gesetz*) on Spinoza (*Omnis determinatio est negatio*) – G. W. F. Hegel, *Wissenschaft der Logik*, vol. 1 (ed. Lasson, Hamburg 1971) p. 100

[26]This notion is developed at length in *Midrash Temurah*, printed in Jellinek, *Beit HaMidrash*, vol. 1 (reprint Jerusalem 1967) p.106: "Everything has a partner, an opposite, without which it would not be: Why is Life called Life, and why is Death called Death? Without Death, it would not be called Life, and it would not be known that it was Life. Similarly Death: Without Life, it would not be called Death, and it would not be known that it was Death." Wisdom and Foolishness, Righteousness and Wickedness, Purity and Impurity all receive similar treatment.

exists, nothing can be known.[27] Similarly, in the lower depths of Judgement, there is a place of darkness where "there is no light nor any darkness, and no image at all. In that place there is no knowledge at all for there is no form which could be considered a real impression."[28]

In the extremes of light (above) and darkness (below) nothing can exist – for finite form requires a balance between the extremes of identity and difference, just as a visual image requires a balance between light and dark in order to be seen. The balance between Judgement and Mercy, which in rabbinic sources was considered necessary in order for the world to stand, receives an ontological twist here: the balance between Judgement and Mercy, the balance between identity and difference, is now considered necessary for the possibility of existence itself.

§10: The Opposition of Judgement and Mercy as a Relative Truth

Harmony and Antagonism, Spirituality and Corporeality, Identity and Difference, as well as the original rabbinic concepts of Forgiveness and Wrath, all seem to represent pairs of antithetical, contradictory principles. On the other hand, the finite world seems to exist only by virtue of their balanced and harmonious interaction. Some kabbalistic sources close to the Zohar were particularly sensitive to the logical problem which this immediate combination of contradictory principles involved:

> Know that among all the Holy Names ... there is not a single attribute of Mercy which does not have in it a little of the attribute of Judgement, nor a single attribute of Judgement which does not have in it a little of the attribute of Mercy ... for if you were to say that the attribute of Mercy is pure Mercy, it would never unite with the pure attribute of Judgement – they would be like *two opposites that could never approach each other*, and if they could not unite, then the Unity [of the Name] would separate into distinct elements – the attribute of Mercy by itself and the attribute of Judgement by itself. (Shaare Orah pp.233-234)

---

[27] Zohar vol. 1 15a
[28] Zohar vol. 1 40a

This text is unwilling to posit an absolute opposition between Judgement and Mercy. He nevertheless defines them as opposites. How can one conceive of relativizing the opposition of opposites?

Within the context of the conceptual framework outlined above, this is not as difficult as it might seem – for opposition (Judgement) was just *one* of the logical principles governing reality. The other principle, Mercy, represents the antithesis of opposition: *the resolution of opposition* and *the transcendence of limitation*.

No one would deny that in the realm of the physical world, which receives the full imprint of Strife, the law of non-contradiction (logical opposition), is inviolable. But in the realm of spiritual beings, which receive the full imprint of Mercy, these absolute oppositions do not necessarily hold.

If Mercy can resolve the opposition between distinct concepts, even between antithetical concepts like righteousness and wickedness – if in Mercy ultimately all notions are unified together as one, then within Mercy, *perhaps even the opposition between Judgement and Mercy is itself overcome.* This is the very conclusion which the Zohar draws.

**Synthesis**

§11: The Dialectic of Judgement and Mercy

If paradox is a characteristic of truth, then we are now approaching the truth of the Divine Name, for the concept of the Divine Name is highly paradoxical. At the same time, the Divine Name, which is essentially defined as Mercy, is a simple concept, as simple and as paradoxical as human love itself:

a. Divine Love, as the primary manifestation of Mercy, overcomes all opposition. It rejects and excludes nothing. It is therefore infinite and includes all within itself.

b. If love were to exclude opposition from itself, it would not be truly infinite, for it would remain opposed to, and limited by opposition. Love must therefore also include opposition within itself.

c. If love were to include opposition within itself merely as part of its own infinity, then the specific character of opposition (its being different and distinct from love itself) would not have been included within love, and love would remain limited and finite. Therefore, in order to be truly infinite, love must include opposition within itself, and at the same time posit opposition as separate and distinct from itself.

d. The only way in which love can do this is by reduplicating itself. Only if Divine love first allows opposition (finitude) to exist beside love (the infinite), and then overcomes the opposition between them by entering into a love relationship with it, does it cease to be the abstract notion of love, and become real love – by becoming the love of two lovers.

e. Divine love must restrain its tendency to overcome opposition in order to allow finitude to exist outside itself. It must then express its tendency to overcome opposition by integrating finitude itself into a higher order of infinity – an infinity which encompasses both the finite and the infinite.

f. If this all encompassing unity could be imposed upon finitude by God, then finitude would have lost its independence, and no higher all encompassing reality would have been achieved. This unity cannot be achieved by God's one sided love alone, but rather only if finitude itself enters into a love relation with God, by freely loving God in return. The corollary to this conclusion is that, like the human lover, the price God pays for the possibility of love is the threat of betrayal – for freedom to love God is also freedom to reject Him.

g. Ultimately God's fate is in human hands: if Man chooses to love God, then God's aspirations as lover are fulfilled – Man and God are integrated into a unity of love (in which Man does not cease to be finite.) If Man rejects God, then Man is separated from God, and finitude ceases to be an expression of God's goodness and infinity – the Indwelling is driven from the world.

## SYNTHESIS

The concept of human love as a free relationship between two lovers is understood *intuitively* to be a higher form of perfection than the love of any solitary lover – certainly higher than any form of compelled love. Similarly, God's infinite love is incomplete so long as it does not manifest itself as real love between God and the finite world, which stands freely outside Him.

### §12: The Four Letters of the Divine Name as Hypostases of this Dialectic

The Zohar's theology reflects both paradoxical root intuitions and fluid modes of thinking about them. It is therefore no wonder that the Zohar, in contradistinction to almost all other kabbalistic thinkers, prefers to avoid static symbols, fixed conceptual categories, and the abstract oppositions which usually accompany them.[29] He prefers to draw pictures of his ideas, moving images of eternity, which can convey the complex reflexive relations which hold between the intimately interconnected concepts. *The Secrets of the Letters* is no exception, and in it, too, the various ideas and images flow into and out of one another constantly.

At the same time he recognizes the need to hypostatize these dynamic processes in symbolic form, if only in order to provide some few fixed sign posts for finding one's way through the maze of his involuted thought. In *the Secrets of the Letters*, the four letters of the Divine Name *YHVH* play this role.

In the following brief text, which reviews the role of these four letters in the creation of the world, each letter acts as a *hypostasis* of some aspect of the dynamic process described above:

> There were a thousand worlds before this world was created. The splendor of His glory extended, and He created worlds and destroyed them – until it arose in His Will to create this world. At that time, two letters from His Name extended, to which He gave permanent existence. Two others were engraved above and below, one within the other. (ZHM 5a)

---

[29]Cf. Tishbi, *Mishnat HaZohar* p.137. Tishbi, following Scholem (*Major Trends* pp.212–214) expects the Zohar to describe the ten familiar Sephirot emanating neatly one after the other in order. When this doesn't occur, he ascribes this to a lack of consistency on the part of the Zohar. In our view, the Zohar's thought is consistent, but because of its fluid and dialectical character it can be symbolized in various ways.

The Name, as Mercy, was seen to include Judgement within it. But the inclusion of Judgement was twofold: first, as contained implicitly within the concept of Mercy itself; second, as manifest Judgement, distinct from the concept of Mercy. The four letters of the Divine Name provide the *symbolic framework* for these various aspects, as they emerge from the concept of Mercy.

The first two letters, *Yod* and *He,* were already seen (§8) to represent Mercy and Judgement. In *the Secrets of the Letters,* these two letters are *engraved one within the other,* as in the text cited here. They represent the concept of Mercy *(Yod)* which includes Judgement *(He)* implicitly, but in which Judgement finds no explicit expression. This hidden Judgement is however the *root* or *source* of Judgement, which eventually finds full manifestation in the finite world. Following the notion (§9) that finite form derives from the opposition of one distinct entity to another, neither *Yod* nor *He* achieves permanent existence, because Mercy and Judgement are not yet distinguished from each other at this stage.

The second two letters, *Vav* and *He,* are parallel to the first two letters. *Vav* represents Mercy and *He* represents Judgement. They represent the unity of Mercy and Judgement in the form of a balance between opposition and unity. In this balance Judgement *posits* and Mercy *resolves* opposition, without either getting the upper hand. These two letters, *Vav* and *He,* are identified, both in *the Secrets of the Letters*[30] and elsewhere in the Zohar, with the Bride and Bridegroom of *the Song of Songs* – for human love is itself an expression of this same balance between opposition and unity.

### §13: The Transcendent Creator

According to the Zohar, before it *arose in His Will to create this world, God and His Name were one.*[31] It is the unequivocal position of the Zohar that the creation of the world, starting from the revelation of the four letters of his Name, was the result of a free act of Divine will. On the other hand, finite reality seems to emerge *neces-*

---

[30]SLDN 1.392 ff.
[31]ZHM 5a; cf. Pirke Rabbi Eliezer ch.3.

*sarily* from the dialectic of Mercy and Judgement which the Name represents. If the Name was included within God from all eternity, why isn't the existence of the finite world, which seems to follow from it, also necessarily eternal?

The concept of Mercy, as interpreted above, dissolves the opposition and specificity which is posited by Judgement. By extension the notion of *absolute Mercy* would dissolve *all* opposition, *all* specificity, and so all manifestation of Judgement. The concept of Mercy included in the Name, which was analyzed above, is not this absolute Mercy, for it includes some manifestation of Judgement. But it points to another more radical notion of Mercy – the infinite Mercy of the Creator, which, by resolving all opposition and all distinctions, is beyond all thought.

Aristotle set down in his law of non-contradiction that the denial of logical opposition between contrary concepts destroys all possibility of thought or speech.[32] Translated into the Zohar's terminology, this means that thought exists only where Judgement is manifest. Even if the infinity of the Creator is assumed to include Judgement, any manifestation of its power would be absolutely suppressed. With the absolute suppression of logical opposition, all notions of necessary inference would likewise disappear.

When the concept of the Name is analyzed, Judgement emerges from the dialectical concept of Mercy. This inference, like all inferences, follows *only* if there is already some manifestation of Judgement.[33] But before creation, all logical specificity, including that of the Name, is dissolved within the Creator. Since all manifestation of Judgement is suppressed, there is no possibility of logical inference, *and so nothing follows necessarily.*

---

[32]Cf. *Metaphysics* 1006a ff.

[33]This is the meaning of the Zohar's insistence that all the distinctions which we make within the Name are "from our perspective". See Zohar vol. 2 176a and vol. 3 141b. Scholem (*Major Trends* p.224 note 66) interprets this not as an ontological distinction between levels or aspects of being, but as if it were limiting the reality of these phenomena to the realm of human subjectivity. This unnecessarily complicated Scholem's argument, whose basic understanding is substantially in accord with our interpretation.

## THE CONCEPT OF THE DIVINE NAME

Of the Transcendent Creator nothing can be said. It cannot be said that He is Mercy, since Mercy has a specific content — the resolution of distinction. It cannot even be said of Him that He is the *collapse of Mercy and Judgement* into each other, as could be said of letters *Yod* and *He*. *Yod* and *He* represent aspects of the revealed Name in which Mercy and Judgement are distinguished. Therefore, even if their unity (in which all distinction is cancelled) cannot itself be defined, it may be grasped *indirectly* as the coalescence of two specific entities which may be defined.[34] But of the Holy One, blessed be He, one cannot speak even indirectly, for He is not connected, either causally or logically, to anything which can be grasped.

### §14: Tsimtsum

The concept of *Tsimtsum*, Divine *self-limitation*, is usually associated with the later developments of Lurianic Kabbalah.[35] In fact, both the concept and the term itself seem to have their roots in the earliest texts of the Zohar itself.[36] The term *Tsimtsum* in the Zohar designates God's initial creative act, an act which of necessity occurs within God Himself. It is this first act of creation which

---

[34] This type of knowledge is termed *speculative* by Hegel. See G. W. F. Hegel, Enzyklopadie §82. In the *Zusatz* at the end of this section, Hegel discusses the meaning of the term *mystical*, and its relation to rational knowledge. With respect to the Name, I would agree with Hegel, as against Scholem (*Major Trends* p.225), that the mystical theology of the Zohar is only mysterious from the limited perspective of *Verstand*, whereas from the enlightened perspective of *Vernunft*, the mysteries are revealed — they are intelligible. However as regards the Transcendent Creator, even the speculative knowledge of *Vernunft* fails. Hegel, as a consistent rationalist, rejects the notion of an Unknown Transcendent. See his critique of kabbalistic and Gnostic thought in his *Lectures on the History of Philosophy*, part 1, section 3B.

[35] *Major Trends* p.260 ff. and G. Scholem, "Schopfung aus Nichts und Selbstverschrankung Gottes," in *Uber einige Grundbegriffe des Judentums* (Frankfurt am Main 1970) pp. 84–89.

[36] Rabbi Aryeh Kaplan tried to point out traces of this doctrine in earlier kabbalistic sources in his edition of *Sefer HaBahir* (New York 1979 p.xv). But he unnecessarily weakened his case by relying upon proof-texts which merely *hint* at the notion of *Tsimtsum*, instead of dealing with it explicitly, and by using authoritative (Lurianic!) commentaries to interpret these texts, instead of showing how the doctrine is reflected in the texts themselves.

## SYNTHESIS

allows the Name, and with it the finite world, to emerge from out of the infinity of the Transcendent Creator.

Because of its inherent interest and its importance for our discussion here, we will quote the relevant passages at length:

> Rabbi Yehuda said: "Let the waters be gathered together." Like the line which the craftsman employs when building a building, so that it should not extend too far in any direction, so also God made a line for the waters, so that they should not extend beyond their border in any direction ... It is taught: The Holy One, blessed be He, established a boundary for the sea. What is this boundary? Rabbi Abba said: This is the Sand, as it is written, "who set the sand as a boundary to the sea." (Jer. 5.22) When they see the sand they turn back, and they do not extend beyond that line which the Holy One, blessed be He, established for them. Rabbi Yitzhak said: Come and see how much the essence of the world is water, for even the heavens take their name from it – *mayim* (water) *sha-mayim* (heaven). Why? Rabbi Yitzhak said: Because the Holy One, blessed be He, added fire to the water and created from them heaven – that is to say *esh* (fire) and *mayim* (water). (ZHM 21b)

Thus far, the passage consists of a series of quite ordinary midrashim. However, the passage which immediately follows radically alters the perspective from which these midrashim must be viewed:

> Rabbi Yehudai said: That cannot be, for the heavens were created from the Love which is before the Holy One, blessed be He! Rabbi Elazar said: Rabbi Yitzhak has spoken well, and it does not contradict that which Rabbi Yehudai has said, for when you know the true meaning of *water*, you will know the true essence of the matter. (Ibid)

The Zohar, in a rather heavy-handed fashion, has instructed us to read these texts *symbolically*. He sets up one symbolic equivalence explicitly. Given this clue it is not difficult to decifer the rest. If Water = Love (Mercy), then it is certain that Fire is a symbol for Judgement. Heaven, which is made up of the two together, is a symbol for the synthesis of Mercy and Judgement represented by the letter *vav*.[37]

According to the verse under consideration (Gen. 1.9), the waters were gathered together so that the *dry land* might appear. Given the

---

[37]Cf. §23 below and SLDN ll.550-551

symbolic interpretation of the first half of the verse, what is the "true meaning" of the Dry Land which is first revealed by the limitation and restriction of the Waters?

> Rabbi Yitzhak said: At that time, the waters took the earth that was contained within them, and they covered it over. The Holy One, blessed be He, said to them, "Not thus! Rather gather together to one place, and let the dry land be seen!" This implies that the earth had already been dry land without moisture among the waters. It does not say "dry land", but rather "*the* dry land". (ZHM 22a)

This image of Dry Land is a standard symbol in the Zohar for the final letter *he* of the Divine Name (§12), which represents the full manifestation of Judgement. This Judgement was already pre-existent within God before creation, but it was hidden by the waters until they were restricted to one place.

Slightly further on, the Zohar puts a description of this primordial act of limitation (*Tsimstum*) into the mouth of King David, who addresses God in the following words:

> David said: You are He who made the entire world, and you made the waters. The waters engulfed the entire world because of their vastness. You forced them to gather together in *Tsimstum*, all of them to one place. (Ibid)

Through the *Tsimtsum* of the infinite waters of Mercy, the Dry Land of Judgement appears, and with it the finite world. Judgement, limitation, and finitude are waiting to be expressed. It is the infinity of God's Mercy which prevents this expression. If these waters are restrained through *Tsimtsum*, Judgement will emerge automatically.

*Tsimtsum* is not the source of the reality of finite being, but rather Judgement is. *Tsimtsum* merely allows the pre-existent Judgement to emerge. The Judgement which emerges is a direct expression of God's own innermost being. At the same time it is the source of all opposition to God, both the relative opposition of finitude and the absolute opposition of evil.

The process of creation, as understood by the Zohar, sets up a complex relationship between God and the world, a dialectical movement of opposition and reconciliation which does not fit well into the standard conceptual categories of *pantheism* or *theism*.³⁸ The contradictions which result from attempts to force the Zohar's thought into one or the other of these categories do not reflect any inconsistency on the part of the Zohar, but rather the conceptual inadequacy of the categories themselves.

### §15: The Transcendent Source of Evil

The notion of an all inclusive Divine Mercy may resolve the logical tensions between the concepts of Judgement and Mercy. But it only makes the moral problematics of the rabbinic theological tradition more severe.³⁹ If the infinity of the Creator includes all within itself, then even infinite negativity – evil itself – must find its source in God. This of course is no innovation. Traditional Jewish monotheism, whether biblical or rabbinic, would never admit the existence of a second evil power in competition with the good and merciful God of Israel. The added difficulty here lies in the intimate identification of this principle of evil with God's own being.

There are a number of important texts in the Zohar where the source and nature of evil are discussed at great length.⁴⁰ *The Secrets of the Letters* is not one of them. It focuses its attention almost exclusively upon the *side of holiness*, and touches upon *the other side, the side of impurity*, only in passing. For this reason, an extended analysis of the problem should be put off until one or more of these other texts can be examined in detail.

Nevertheless, included in the very notion of the *side of holiness* is the integration of Judgement into the unity of the Divine Name, and its transformation from a destructive principle of evil into a good and just source of finite existence. This aspect is essential to the story which is told in *the Secrets of the Letters*, and so it will be necessary to make a few anticipatory remarks on the subject, based on the conceptual outline developed in the preceding sections.

---

³⁸Cf. *Major Trends* p.38

³⁹See §§4 and 5 above

⁴⁰The most important passages are: vol. 2 242b–244b and 262b–268b. A briefer presentation of the basic elements can be found in vol. 1 16a.

Suppose, as was suggested above, that the infinity of the Creator includes infinite negativity, Absolute Judgement, within itself. Assuming that the Absolute Mercy of the Creator is capable of resolving even Absolute Judgement, then before creation even this Absolute Negativity could have been hidden and dissolved within the infinity of God's Mercy. With *Tsimtsum*, the finitude implicit in the Name becomes manifest. What of the Absolute Judgement which had previously been dissolved within God's Absolute Mercy – does it remain above, safely neutralized?

The Zohar's understanding of this process is not so favorable. In his view it is precisely the harsh, evil Judgement which is first to emerge,[41] and for good reason. There is no antagonism and opposition to God's Mercy like the infinite opposition of Absolute Judgement. If anything is to stand opposed to and outside of God's Mercy, it would be this. It is only the absolute suppression of opposition itself which prevents these two from separating from and re3pelling each other even before creation. With the first limitation of Mercy, and the first nascent expression of negativity, the Absolute Darkness of Judgement is the first to escape from its captivity, to flee to the furthest extremes of the universe – to set up its own realm, *the other side of impurity*.

After this initial emergence of darkness and opposition, the process of *reintegrating* this darkness into the light of Mercy begins. The Zohar describes this process using a number of different images. In the Idra Rabba, the initial emergence of Judgement is described in the following way: "Some were sweetened, some were sweetened and not sweetened – some were not sweetened at all." [42] The harsh Judgement which emerged had to be reintegrated into the unity and holiness of creation. This process is called "the sweetening of Judgement".[43] Some aspects of negativity could be immediately and totally integrated, others only partially integrated. Some remained outside of the realm of holiness altogether.

---

[41] See for example Zohar vol. 1 12a.

[42] Zohar vol. 3 135b

[43] See *Major Trends* p.165 note 44.

Elsewhere, this process is described as the *sifting* of the good grain out of the chaff with which it was intermingled. The worthless residue which remains after all that is positive has been sifted out is called "refuse." [44] In *the Secrets of the Letters*, this worthless residue is referred to by its more ominous and familiar name: the burning darkness of *Gehinnom*, of Hell.[45] There is no need to describe here the process of reintegrating this darkness into the light of Mercy, since this dealt with at length in *the Secrets of the Letters*, and will be analysed in detail below.

**Structure and Symbol**

The emergence of Judgement (the Divine Name) out of the infinite Mercy of the Transcendent Creator is represented schematically in kabbalistic literature in different ways. If the Transcendent Creator is represented as a fixed point, then the process of the progressive emergence of Judgement is a linear motion away from that point. If the Transcendent Creator is pictured as filling all space, then this process may be represented as the progressive motion inward toward a finite point, as in the Kabbalah of the Ari.[46]

*The Secrets of the Letters* adopts a number of models for depicting this motion, all of which are basically in line with the first option – the Infinite is pictured *above*, and emergence of finitude is *linear progression downward*. The three most prominent sets of concrete images used in this description are taken from the fields of Orthography, Mathematics, and Optics.

---

[44]Zohar vol.1 16a

[45]SLDN ll. 207–209

[46]Cf. *Etz Haim* 11b ff. The very notion of conceptual *motion*, as used, for example, in Hegel's Logic, is itself a metaphor, taken from this kind of concrete representation. For the origins of this notion of conceptual motion, see Sambursky and Pines, *The Concept of Time in Late Neoplatonism* (Jerusalem 1987) pp.12–17.

§16: Orthographic Symbols

Most of the orthographic symbols in *the Secrets of the Letters* are modeled on the concrete image of the Written Torah (the Five Books of Moses) itself. Earlier Kabbalists had already reported a tradition to the effect that the entire Written Torah can be understood as a collection of Names of God. According to the earlier understanding, this tradition refers to an *esoteric* reading of the Torah which redivides the unpunctuated Hebrew text into alternative word groupings which differ from the familiar traditional word divisions.[47] In this way the ordinary exoteric sense of the Torah text may be transmuted into an object of mystical contemplation.

The Zohar's understanding of this tradition is very different, reflecting a position close to that expressed in the following passage:

> Know that all of His Holy Names which are mentioned in the Torah are dependent upon *the four letter Name* which is *YHVH* .... It is like the trunk of a tree ... and the rest of the *Holy Names* are like the branches ... which extend from the trunk of the tree .... Aside from the *Holy Names* which it is forbidden to erase, there are many *descriptive terms*, dependent upon each Name ... while all these *descriptive terms* have other *descriptive terms*, which are dependent upon them, and they are all the *words* in the Torah. So it turns out that all the Torah is woven upon the *descriptive terms*, and the descriptive terms upon the *Names*, and the *Holy Names* are all dependent upon the Name *YHVH*, and are all unified in it. (Shaare Orah p.48)

This approach starts from the exoteric reading of the Torah text, and categorizes the various words according to their literal sense. A descriptive term like *merciful* represents an aspect of Mercy. This attribute is itself represented in the Torah by the Holy Name *El*. So the term *merciful* will be placed under the heading of *El*. Alternatively, a word like *blessing*, or a sentence like "God remembered his covenant," may also have a certain literal content which corresponds to an aspect of some Holy Name. The noun *blessing* might be connected to the Divine attribute of *goodness*, while *remembering His covenant* might be connected to the attribute of *faithfulness*.

---

[47]Nachmanides, *Commentary on the Torah*, vol.1 (Jerusalem 1959) pp. 6–7

Since this approach starts from the literal sense of the Torah text, and since not all words refer to God's Name with the same degree of *immediacy*, it is possible to set up a hierarchy of terms, depending on the immediacy or remoteness with which they are related to God. The Name *YHVH* is the most immediate expression of God's creative and providential power. The other Holy Names, like *El, Elohim, Adonai*, are intimately connected to God Himself, but their relation to Him is mediated by the Name *YHVH*. Below the Holy Names are *attributes – descriptive terms* like *kind, merciful, judge, awesome, mighty*.[48]

While *Shaare Orah* models the progressive branching out of Names, attributes, and words on the organic image of a tree, the *Secrets of the Letters* adopts an abstract model like those mentioned above. Moreover it takes the process behind the level of *Names*, back to the level of *Letters* – even to the abstract level of *Marking* and *Impression* which is the necessary presupposition of writing itself:

a. The first orthographic image which is employed in *the Secrets of the Letters* is *Impression* or *Marking*. It could either refer to the act of making a recognizable mark on parchment, or perhaps even to the act of making straight lines upon parchment in preparation for the eventual act of writing intelligible script upon it.[49]

b. Upon this impression, *Letters* are written. Throughout the entire first section of *the Secrets of the Letters* only the first two letters of the Name YHVH are mentioned, but no Holy Names.

c. Below this, *Holy Names* emerge, like YHVH, El, and Elohim, which reflect explications of aspects of the letters.

d. Below each Holy Name, there are *descriptive terms*, like merciful, holy, strong, etc.

---

[48]For more comprehensive and graphic illustrations of this approach see *Shaare Orah* pp. 220–221, 243, and 256.

[49]See SLDN notes to line 4

The motion proceeds from unity to multiplicity, and from vague undefined entities to well defined terms with specific meanings. This pattern will return again in the following sets of symbols.

### §17: Mathematical Symbols

The symbolism of numbers and geometrical space plays a major role in the *Book of Creation*, an important source for the imagery of *the Secrets of the Letters*. These and similar images were further developed by the generations of Kabbalists which preceded the Zohar. There are many different mathematical images in *the Secrets of the Letters*. The following selection is no more than an outline:

a. The highest mathematical image is the *Infinite*. Related to it is the notion of the *Primordial Measuring*, which marks the first introduction of Limit into the Unlimited.

b. Out of these, the *Primordial Point* emerges. The notion of a point stands midway between infinity and finitude, in that it is limited, yet lacks finite dimension.

c. The word which is then applied to this point is *Extension:* a mathematical term which refers to spacial extension, as in the extension of a point into a line, or a line into a plane. It introduces the first element of finite dimension.[50]

d. Next comes the beginnings of the spacial opposition of *Left* and *Right*.

e. Finally, the full range of *Spacial Dimensions* develops, either in the image of the four directions of the World (North, South, East, West) or the six dimensions (NSEW, plus Up and Down).

The progression of these images is from *above to below*. The motion is clearly from unity to multiplicity, from infinity to finite

---

[50]In a related passage (ZHM 81b) the order is as follows: A single Point extends in three directions. This one Point puts forth Three Points. A Measuring Line is then drawn which connects the Points to each other.

measure, and from lack of spacial distinction and opposition to the full development of spacial distinction and opposition.

## §18: Optical Symbolism

In *the Secrets of the Letters*, light imagery is by far the most developed of the three representations of the vertical chain of Being.

a. The first light image is the *Lamp* – the unitary source of all further derivative lights.

b. Out of the Lamp, a singular *Sparkling* emerges.

c. From this sparkling, *multiple Sparks* emerge.

d. The totality of sparks coalesce into a single *Light*.

e. Out of this *Light, multiple Lights* emerge, which are not distinguished by different colors.

f. At this point, the opposition of *Light* to *Darkness* is introduced.

g. From the Light, *manifold lights with different colors* emerge.

h. From the Darkness, *manifold shades and colors of darkness* emerge.

The motion of these stages is always downward, away from the Lamp. As the lights move downward, they change from *sparks*, to *undefined lights*, to *distinct colors*, while the number of distinct lights always grows larger. The motion here too is from unity to multiplicity, from infinity to finitude, with the addition of qualitative opposition (color), to the already familiar quantitative imagery.

## §19: Chariot and Support

There are two other important symbols which are used throughout *the Secrets of the Letters* for the emergence of multiplicity and finitude: *Chariot* and *Support*.

The concrete imagery of the Divine Chariot (Ez. chp.1) was highly developed in ancient Jewish mystical and midrashic literature. There are a number of passages in the Zohar where the highly colorful images of *Ofanim, Serafim,* the multiple faces and wings of the *Holy Beasts* which carry the Divine Chariot are employed, and even elaborated further.[51] In *the Secrets of the Letters,* only the term Chariot itself appears, without any of this accompanying imagery. It seems to be used in the following abstract sense: just as a king's chariot is a vehicle for and symbol of his majesty and power, so also the various entities which emerge out of God's transcendent unity are *expressions of* and *symbols for His majesty and power.*

The term Support is taken from the biblical description of the Tabernacle (§22 below). The Tabernacle was attached to the ground by metal rings. These rings fit into the ground, and the planks and beams of the Tabernacle were set into them. In this way, the rings (called *supports* in the Aramaic translation to the Torah text) linked the Tabernacle to the earth and were interposed between them. It is in this abstract sense of *linking* and *mediating between above and below* that the term is used throughout *the Secrets of the Letters.*

§20: Syntax

Throughout *the Secrets of the Letters,* the Zohar employs a fixed vocabulary in conjunction with the concrete images described in the last four sections. This vocabulary of verbs, adjectives, and adverbs ties together the disjointed concrete images used in any given passage, which are frequently drawn from unrelated lists. It is the glue which builds the isolated elements of the Zohar's symbolism into a coherent series of propositions. The following is a selection of the most common words:

  a. *obscure* – literally *closed*; it can also mean *implicit* or *indefinite.* It is opposed to *explicit* or *definite.* The common verb *itp'rash* is derived from the word *explicit,* and means *to differentiate* or *to become distinct.* The more rare verb *istim* is

---

[51]For example ZHM 62b–68b and Zohar vol. 1 41a ff.

derived from the word *obscure*, and means *to become indistinct*, and for that reason unknowable.

b. *hidden (inaccessible) / revealed (accessible)* – Obscure elements are inherently unknowable since they have no discernable form. For this reason, they are called *hidden*, or more rarely *inaccessible*. Distinct, well defined elements, on the other hand, may be known, and so are termed *revealed*, or *accessible*.

c. *above / below / connected* – The *obscure* and *indistinct* elements are depicted as being *above*, and the more *well defined* elements are depicted as being *below*. They are *connected* or *tied* to each other, presumably by logical or causal links.

d. *emerge / put forth* – The lower elements *emerge* from those above them; these higher elements *put forth* those which emerge below them.

e. *ascend / descend* – When tracing the interconnection of elements upward, these elements are said to *ascend*; when tracing this interconnection downward, they are said to *descend*.

## §21: Symbols of Opposition and Unity

As the elements descend in this linear model, there is increasing internal differentiation between the elements themselves. At a certain stage in the process, shades of darkness are distinguished from different colors of light. Spacial oppositions like North versus South emerge. Among the *descriptive terms*, opposing categories of forgiveness and punishment begin to form. This signifies the progressive differentiation of Judgement from Mercy. In order to depict the dialectic of Mercy and Judgement which develops at this point, the Zohar employs symbols which represent in concrete form the same balance of unity and opposition which is found in the dialectic.

The first model is the organic unity of the *human body* itself. In rabbinic literature, the Attribute of Mercy is identified with God's *right hand*, while the the Attribute of Judgement is identified with God's *left hand*:

> "Your right hand, YHVH, glorious in power." (Ex.15.6) – When Israel does God's will, they make *left into right* ... but when they do not do God's will, they make *right into left*, as it is written, "He has withdrawn His right hand." (Lam.2.3) (MRI p.134)

In the continuation of this text (cited in §5 above), this notion of turning *right into left* is explicated further: it means arousing God's unmitigated wrath, *making the Merciful cruel*. God's right hand is his Mercy, his left Judgement. When the right is withdrawn, and no longer restrains the wrath of the left hand of Judgement, then cruel and harsh punishment emerges.

The notion of Mercy and Judgement as the two hands of God carries with it an implicit notion of unity – for hands are joined organically within the unity of a single body. It is not clear to what extent the role of the *body* as mediating between the two extremes of God's *left* and *right hands* is recognized in rabbinic literature. But in the Zohar the rabbinic pair, *left* and *right*, becomes a trio: the *right* and *left hands* (or *arms*) of Mercy and Judgement as opposites, and the *body* which represents the unity of Mercy and Judgement. The body as a whole, including the opposing limbs, represents the dialectical balance between unity and opposition.[52]

A further rabbinic development of this imagery introduces a second important model for this dialectic: the *balance scale*:

> "And all the heavenly host standing before Him to His right and to His left." (1K22.19) – Is there indeed *left* above?! Is not everything *right* [above], as it is written, "Your right hand, YHVH, glorious in power, your right hand, YHVH, shatters the foe." So what is the meaning of *to His right and to His left?* [Rather it refers to] those [angels] who incline to the right and those who incline to the left – those who *tip the scales in favor of innocence*, and those who *tip the scales in favor of guilt*.[53]

This text identifies the images of *left hand* and *right hand* with Judgement and Mercy, as in the text cited above. But the presenta-

---

[52]Cf. SLDN 1.462 ff.

[53]Song of Songs Rabbah 1:9.1; see also Zohar vol. 3 129b bottom.

tion here differs substantially from that of the previous text. There, God was described as having two hands. The verse *(Your right hand, YHVH)* was interpreted as saying that when God's right hand is withdrawn, it no longer restrains His left hand. This only reinforces the concrete anthropomorphic image. Here the verse, *Your right hand, YHVH*, etc., is cited to prove that God has no left hand at all, for there is only *right* above.

This transformation is important in two respects. First, left and right are beginning to be used *abstractly* to represent Judgement and Mercy. Without left in its ordinary spacial sense, there will be no right. So the statement *there is only right above* must be construed as the equivalent of *there is only Mercy above* – the term *right* having lost most of its concrete anthropomorphic sense. Secondly, the notion that the struggle between the competing forces of Judgement and Mercy only emerges *below*, while *above* all is depicted as Mercy, is consonant with, and constitutes a precedent for, the schematic hierarchy of Being which was outlined in the previous sections.

However, the text also extends this imagery in a new direction. Inclining toward Mercy is depicted as *tipping the scales* in favor of innocence, while inclining toward Judgement is depicted as *tipping the scales* in favor of guilt. The *balance scale* is a particularly appropriate symbol for the dialectic of Judgement and Mercy. The left side weighs down in favor of punishment, and only in favor of punishment. The right side inclines the scales only in the direction of forgiveness. Yet together they counterbalance each other, producing measured, fair judgement. It is the central balance which decides between them, bringing these opposites together in harmonious cooperation. In its Aramaic form, *matkela*, the balance scale becomes a central, perhaps *the* central image of the dialectic of Judgement and Mercy in the Zohar.[54]

## §22: Tabernacle Symbolism

In *the Secrets of the Letters*, there is a particularly dense family of symbols for the unity of Mercy and Judgement which is drawn from

---

[54]E.g. Zohar vol. 2 176b in *Sifra deTsniuta;* also the *Book of Creation* 3.1.

one central source: the description of the Tabernacle which the Israelites built in the desert:

> He made bars of acacia wood, five for the planks of the first side of the Tabernacle, and five bars for the planks of the second side of the Tabernacle ... and he made the central bar to pass through them from end to end. (Ex.36.31–33)

The Tabernacle was constructed out of separate planks. Bars ran through the planks, joining them together into two opposing sides. The Zohar understood the final words of this passage to mean that these two opposing sides were themselves joined together by a single central bar which passed through all of them from end to end, despite the fact that this would seem to be structurally impossible.

The Zohar identifies the two opposing sides of the Tabernacle with Mercy and Judgement. The unity of Mercy and Judgement is represented by the central bar, which he calls the *middle side*, on analogy with the two opposing *sides*. (This phrase is also no doubt influenced by the abstract medieval usage of *side* to mean *aspect*.) The *middle side* "takes the two sides to pass through them with bars and doors."[55] This sentence from *the Secrets of the Letters* is taken almost verbatum from the Aramaic Targum to the verses cited above.

The planks of each side of the Tabernacle were placed within metal rings, *supports*, by means of which they were fixed to the ground:

> And for the second side of the Tabernacle, the north side, he made twenty planks with their forty silver supports, two supports under each plank. (Ex.36.25–26)

The Zohar derives another layer of symbols from this passage: if the *second side* (Judgement) is North, then the *first side* (Mercy),

---

[55]SLDN 1.256 ff. The term *doors* seems to be an associative transformation of the Aramaic word for *planks*: *dapin* (planks) into the very similar *dashin* (doors). The term *doors* may have its source in the phrase "the doors of the gate of the East", from the blessings before *Shma* in the Sabbath morning service, which refers to the rising of the Sun, a symbol for letter *vav*. See also Zohar vol. 2 175b top, and *Shekel haKodesh* pp.48–49.

which stands opposite it, is South. The *middle side* is the *Eastern Gate*, for in the Tabernacle the opening in the courtyard was in the middle of the eastern side.

Finally, the relation of the planks to the supports below them provides a concrete model for the progressive differentiation of elements in the descent of the vertical chain of being: just as each plank has two supports below, so also each element differentiates downward, *two to each side.*[56]

### §23: Symbols from Maimonidean Physics

The symbolic significance of the balance scale in the Zohar was outlined above in §21. The *Book of Creation* identified the three parts of the balance scale with the three primary elements, air, fire, and water.[57] This is probably the primary source for the Zohar's use of *fire* and *water* as symbols for Judgement and Mercy as opposites, and *air* as a symbol for their unity. However, the *syntax* which the Zohar employs to define the interpenetration of these elements shows the definite impact of the Aristotelean doctrine of the elements, as presented by Maimonides[58] in the opening chapters of his *Mishneh Torah:*

> These four bodies, which are fire, air, water, and earth, are the elements of all the creatures under the heavens . . . . All four of them mix together . . . and in the mixture there is not the smallest particle which is fire by itself, or water by itself, or earth by itself, or air by itself. *Rather they are all transformed into a single body,* and any body which is composed of these four will have within it cold and hot, moist and dry, all together. However, there are some bodies in which the element of fire predominates . . . and some bodies in which the element of earth predominates . . . and some bodies in which the element of water predominates . . . . The quantity of the element which is the main component of the admixture will determine the behavior and nature of the composite body. (Foundations 4:1-2)

---

[56]Cf. SLDN ll.192–195

[57]*Book of Creation* 3.1

[58]The Zohar's repeated use of the Aramaic term *ittaqaph* for *predominate* in SLDN, shows the direct influence of Maominides' formulation. It is an artificial translation of the Hebrew word *hithazeq*, derived from the word *hazaqah*, which Maimonides uses for *predominate* in the following passage.

This doctrine assumes the existence of two primary pairs of contrary attributes: *cold* and *hot, moist* and *dry*. The four primary elements, *fire, air, earth,* and *water*, are believed to be constituted by these two pairs of contrary attributes: fire is hot and dry, air is hot and moist, water is cold and moist, earth is cold and dry. The doctrine which Maimonides expounds in the passage cited here is an attempt to solve a riddle: how can a cold and dry substance, like wood, burn – giving off hot and dry fire, and hot and moist vapors? Essential qualities cannot simply turn into their opposites. In response to this riddle, Aristotle[59] posited that all physical bodies, which come to be or cease to be, are *composite*: each body *includes* all four elements in varying proportions, but displays only the qualities of that element which *predominates* in the admixture.

These two notions, *inclusion* and *predominance*, play an important role in *the Secrets of the Letters*. This vocabulary is used to describe the interpenetration and unification of the contrary attributes of Mercy and Judgement. However, unlike some Kabbalists who seem to have taken this model literally,[60] the Zohar uses it only as a starting point for expounding his much more subtle dialectical notion of unity.

---

[59]*On Generation and Corruption* 1:9–10 and 2:1–3.
[60]See SLDN notes to line 190.

# THE DOCTRINE OF THE DIVINE NAME

Part Two:

## THE SECRETS OF THE LETTERS OF THE DIVINE NAME

Annotated Translation and Critical Notes

# THE SECRETS OF THE LETTERS OF THE DIVINE NAME
from the Zohar[1]

[Introductory Verses: 1-3]

Rabbi Shimon opened [his discourse]: "Who can tell the mighty acts of the Lord, proclaim all His praises?" (Ps.106.2) "Who would not revere you, O King of the nations? For that is Your due, since among all the wise of the nations and among all their royalty, there is none like you." (Jer.10.7)

[Introduction: 4-8]

Into the obscure[2] letters which are engraved upon the obscurity of the Impression of Existence,[3] chariots ascend, [they ascend] into Holy Chariots. Each chariot ascends into an inscribed letter. That letter is inscribed with its existence. Its chariot ascends into it. Each letter stands upon the existence of the chariot which corresponds to it.[4] From here on, the matter stands ready to be explicated[5] – each letter in the mystery of the Holy Chariots.[6]

## [Letter Yod]

[The Ascent and Descent of Letter Yod: 8-15]

The mystery[7] of the first letter ascends and descends. In its crowns, it ascends toward One Hundred Worlds. Corresponding to this, the letter *yod* ascends into the Will of Thought,

---

[1] *THE SECRETS ... Zohar* – other texts: title missing

[2] *obscure* – other texts read: *inscribed*

[3] *Existence* – or: *Permanence*

[4] *corresponds to it* – literally: *is fitting for it*

[5] *to be explicated* – or: *to differentiate*

[6] *Holy Chariots* – other texts add: [*on the four sides of the world.*]

[7] *mystery* – or: *principle.*

loses its definition and is not known. Below it, a Nut forms, which covers the Hidden with hiddenness.[8] It is the chariot which stands below this hidden mystery, and that letter exists hidden away, a single point. Below it,[9] that Nut stands with six supports, which support it on six sides. They are the Six Sides, hidden away within this Nut.

[The Emergence of the Chariot of Letter Yod: 15–19]

A Holy Chariot[10] emerges from a side[11] of this letter. This chariot is hidden away and not revealed – except when the light of the hidden Nut shines. Then this chariot is revealed, and the chariot becomes [both] hidden and revealed. It emerges out of the sparkling of the Lamp, when the Measuring Line is measured – below the first tip[12] [of letter *yod*].[13]

[The Three Sides of the Chariot of Letter Yod: 19–27]

When the Measuring Line exists, the sparkling shines – it ascends and descends, and forms a support below letter *yod* on another side.[14] Afterwards, the sparkling extends, and puts forth three other sparks, which form supports below the lower tip of *yod*.

---

[8]*Below it ... with hiddenness* – In *Ketem Paz* this sentence reads: *It forms a covering below a single Nut which covers the Hidden with hiddenness.*

[9]*and that letter ... point. Below it* – In *Ketem Paz* this sentence is parsed differently, yielding the reading: *That letter stands in the hiddenness of a single point below it*

[10]*A Holy Chariot* – ZC reads: *One Holy Word*

[11]*a side* – or: *an aspect.* Later texts read: *the secret*

[12]*first tip* – other texts read: *first knot*

[13]*below the first tip [of letter yod]* – ZHM adds here: *[and it is one sparkling.]* Ketem Paz reads: *... when the Measuring Line is measured. Below the first knot [of letter yod], one sparkling emerges.*

[14]*on another side* – other texts read: *and it is a single point*

## LETTER YOD

Afterwards, out of the second knot, another sparkling emerges, which shines, ascends and descends, and forms a support below letter *yod* on another side. Afterwards, that sparkling extends, and puts forth three other sparks which form supports below letter *yod* on this side.

Afterwards, out of the third knot, another sparkling emerges. Through this, the mystery of Sand[15] is tied to the Measuring Line of the Lamp.

[Summary: 28–31]

In consequence, letter *yod*, the upper point, is found to possess nine supports upon which it rests. These constitute the chariot of this letter. Thereupon it shines and, resting upon these nine supports, eight others shine forth from it. All these belong to[16] the mystery of letter *yod*, the hidden upper point.

[The Names of the Three Sides: 32–42]

These nine supports may be defined by names, yet may not be defined by names, because those nine which are called the Infinite[17] exist, yet do not exist, and are not known – they are called [by names] yet not called, and are not known at all. These are defined by names,[18] [in accordance with] the mystery [of the verse]: "before you, I will have compassion upon those whom I will have compassion, and have mercy upon those whom I will have mercy."[19] There is no one who can comprehend them or their names, for they are not revealed

---

[15] *Sand* – or: *The Profane*

[16] *belong to* – literally: *stand in*

[17] *the Infinite* – *Ein Sof*

[18] *defined by names* – other texts add: [*yet are not defined*]

[19] Ex. 33.19 – The Hebrew text contains *nine words*. In the Torah text these nine words are preceded by the words: *I will call the Name YHVH.* These three additional words are added in ZHM.

such that their ways could be comprehended. For this reason, Moses could not comprehend them, because they precede his level. [The words] *before you* refer to that first sparkling.[20] Similarly, all of [the nine supports] exist prior[21] to his level. For this reason,[22] he was not able to comprehend the ways of the Holy One, blessed be He – for they all rise up into Thought, and from there His ways extend in many directions inside the Will of the Holy One, blessed be He (which are not known at all).

## [The First Letter He]

[The Emergence of Letter He: 42–52]

With these supports, this letter ascends upward.[23] The One who strikes (who is unknown) strikes, and the Infinite shines, yet does not shine, and it descends. (It is not known from whom it shines.) When [letter *yod*] descends, these supports are included in it, and it extends. When it extends, a single light emerges, which includes everything. It is[24] enclosed within [this light] like one who has entered into a palace. This palace exists on two sides, enclosed and revealed above. The nine supports shine into this palace, and letter *yod* is hidden away within the palace in those supports. This palace is called *he*, accessible, yet inaccessible, revealed, yet not revealed – not revealed at all. Letter *yod* exists in the mystery [of letter *he*], and also all those supports, because [letter *he*] is hidden, yet everything exists in it to be made manifest.

---

[20] . . .*they precede his level. [The words] "before you" refer to that first sparkling.* – the text in *Ketem Paz* reads: *they precede the level of the first sparkling – concerning it, [the words] "before you" are written.*

[21] *exist prior* – other texts read: *pillars precede*

[22] *For this reason* – early texts read: *All this*

[23] *upward* – MS. S reads: *far, far above*

[24] *It is* – other texts read: *they are*

**FIRST LETTER HE**

[The Chariots of Letter He: 52–58]

[Letter *he*] possesses five chariots which emerge from out of the sparkling of the Lamp when it arrives at its place and is gathered together after it forms[25] the Measuring Line. These [chariots] are called *wonders, fifty* that are *beyond understanding*. King David sought to comprehend these five chariots, as it is written, "Open my eyes, that I may perceive the *wonders* of your Torah." (Ps.119.18) When these [fifty] shine and stand ready to be made manifest,[26] they become[27] five [in order] to shine into five below which emerge from them.[28]

[The Ascent of Letter He: 58–62]

These *fifty* which are *beyond understanding* shine and rise up above it – [there] they are adorned and entwined within those other nine supports. These nine ascend to letter *yod*, far, far above. When they descend (and it is not known from Whom they descend) this *he* is adorned in the mystery of *nun*, which are *fifty*, and *beyond understanding* – which are [also] five supports within it.

[The Descent of Letter He: 62–68]

When it is made manifest[29] and extends, it turns from the mystery of *nun*[30] into the mystery of *he*.[31] These five supports extend downward, and [letter *he*] stands above them.

---

[25] *it forms* – In MS. O these two words are missing.

[26] *stand ready to be made manifest* – or: *rise up above to be adorned*

[27] *they become* – MS. O reads : *it becomes*

[28] *from them* – other texts read: *from it*

[29] *is made manifest* – or: *is adorned*

[30] *nun* – or: *fifty*

[31] *he* – or: *five*

## TRANSLATION

When it fills with all their light – then five other lights emerge from it, which are distinguished [from each other], and yet not distinguished [from each other], with regard to Left and Right. From here on, the matter stands ready to be supported by an upper mystery, in the mystery of the Holy Name. [In this way], one will be enclosed within the other, and the Holy Chariot will be brought to perfection.

### [The Chain of Chariots, from Below to Above: 68–75]

These five [lights] are four. They are five corresponding to the five supports, and they are four corresponding to the four directions of the world. Each [light] has a chariot of its own. Each one of these chariots is included within a single light. Each light is included within those supports. Each support is included in letter *he*. This letter *he* is included in those nine supports. Every one [of these nine supports] is included in letter *yod*, the upper primal point, so that all should be one.

### [Summary of Letter He, Below and Above: 75–80]

Consequently, the chariots which rise up to[32] letter *he*, from below to above, are found to consist of twenty five chariots. This is the mystery of [the verse], "They shall bless You"[33] (Ps.145.10) – from below to above. From letter *he* and above, [there are] nine chariots that stand separately, without number, up to the mystery of letter *yod*, within which all is unknown. From here on, the mystery of the Holy Name becomes manifest in these chariots, so that all should be included, one in the other, in these letters *YHVH*.

---

[32] *rise up to* – or: *which belong to*
[33] *You* – or: *twenty five*

## [The Final Letter He]

[Introductory Verses: 80-83]

Rabbi Shimon said: The Holy One, blessed be He, is called One, as it is written, "YHVH, our God, YHVH is One." (Deut.6.4) The Holy One, blessed be He, is called *First*, as it is written, "I, YHVH, am first." (Is.41.4) The Holy One, blessed be He, is called *Last*, as it is written, "And I am last." (Is.44.6) Blessed be He, and Blessed be his Name forever and for all eternity.

[The Structure of He and its Chariot: 84-93]

The mystery of *And I am last* – this is the final [letter] *he* of the Holy Name, a Holy Chariot which comes last,[34] as it is written, "And with the last ones, I am He." (Is.41.4) *Last* and *Last Ones* – these are all included, one in the other, within a single mystery: the mystery of *five are four*. These *four*, which are[35] the *Last Ones*, all belong both to the upper and lower [worlds].[36] This chariot is *Michael, Gabriel, Rafael, Uriel*. These are *four*[37] – plus the single point which stands above them, they are *five*.[38] They are only called *he* in the mystery of these four and the final point which dwells over them. This is the mystery that this *he* [originally] was *dalet*, but [with] the point which dwells over them in the middle, it became *he*.

---

[34] *comes last* – literally: *is in last*

[35] *which are* – other texts read: *which are called*

[36] *all ... lower [worlds]* – literally: *all exist with respect to above and below*

[37] *four* – or: *[the letter] dalet*

[38] *five* – or: *[the letter] he*

**TRANSLATION**

[The Providential Forces of Letter He – Evil: 93–101]

In the mystery of Enoch, there is another *he* below, which is tied to this *he*. They correspond to each other exactly.[39] Then it is *time to weep*.[40] The sign for this is *ahah*,[41] for [then] all surrounding evil encloses [them] below, in the form of a *dalet*. It surrounds these four and this point, which [then] stands[42] within a hard shell which encloses it. Then the Moon is covered over, its light is enclosed, and permission is given to judge the world with evil judgements. This is the mystery [of the fact] that the second of the two *he*s has a dot[43] [within it], for then judgement is decreed, in the mystery of the verse, "The sentence is decreed by the Watchers, and the verdict is commanded by the Holy Ones, so that . . . ." (Dan.4.14)

[The Providential Forces of Letter He – Good: 101–107]

This chariot belongs to[44] the final [letter] *he*. They never separate from each other. Wherever you find *Michael*,[45] who is the first of these [four], there you will [also] find the *Indwelling*. They are all tied to each other, and they are all tied together within that point – thus it is all *he*. When it is one *he*, and the letter *aleph* or the letter *yod* approach it, and it has the dot [within it], then it comes to benefit the world – *aleph/he* or *yod/he*. For then the evil shell passes away[46] from it, and no longer encloses it.

---

[39]*They . . . exactly* – literally: *They are all one in one.*

[40]*time to weep* – The word *time* is absent in early texts, but the reference is clearly to Eccl. 3.3. Later texts add the word *time* explicitly.

[41]*ahah* (Jer. 1.6) – an *aleph* followed by two *he*s, with a dot in the second *he*

[42]*which [then] stands* – later texts read: *and the point stands*

[43]*a dot* – or: *a point*

[44]*belongs to* – or: *exists in*

[45]*you find Michael* – later texts read: *Michael is found*

[46]*passes away* – or: *is broken*

**FINAL LETTER HE**

[The Inseparability of Letters and Chariots: 107–113]

This [chariot] exists in the mystery [of final letter *he*]. Similarly, every Holy Name (which is one of the Inscribed Letters) possesses a chariot which exists in it, in the Name with respect to which [that chariot] forms a support – and that chariot is its support.[47] For there is no King who travels without his armies, and he is never found alone. Concerning this it is written, "YHVH of Hosts" – all as one, for the chariots do not separate from the Holy Name, and each letter includes its own chariot within it. Thus they all constitute the Holy Name.

[The Inclusion of Lower Powers in the Final Letter He: 113–124]

This letter *he* possesses a chariot among the lower powers. [This is] because letter *he* is revealed.[48] But [you might object that] all of the other letters [also] possess chariots[49] which include their letters in these lower [powers]. [However] only *this* letter (because of this) is included in the *external* lower [powers]; whereas the chariots which are included in the other letters are Holy Chariots, which are not [accessible] to all[50] – except when the palaces join together, the lower [palaces] with the higher [palaces]. But [these lower palaces] are *not* included in these [higher] letters such that they form a single letter. For this reason each letter of the Holy Name contains its chariot

---

[47]*Similarly, every ... is its support.* – This rendering, which is sufficiently convoluted as it stands, is already greatly simplified. A more rigorous translation would read: *Similarly, there is not a single Holy Name among the Inscribed Letters whose chariot does not exist in that letter, in that very Name upon which [said chariot] [the Inscribed Letter] rests, and that [specific] chariot is its support.*

[48]*revealed* – other texts add: [*the least of the companions*]

[49]*chariots* – literally: *a chariot*

[50]*But [you might object] ... not [accessible] to all* – other texts read: *But all the other letters do not have a chariot which includes them in these lower [powers]. Only this one, because this letter is included in the external [powers], while the chariots which are included in the other letters are Holy Chariots, which are not external.*

## TRANSLATION

within it,[51] and this is the Holy Name as is truly fitting. This holds true for each of these four letters. These four letters[52] are the mystery of the chariot for the One who is not known, while each letter has a chariot which is included within it and inscribed in the letter itself.

[The Presence of Upper Mysteries in the Final Letter He: 124–142]

This *he* is *twelve*, and [with] the point which stands above it is *thirteen*. These are the Thirteen Attributes of Mercy below, just like those above. These Thirteen Attributes are *twelve* – the Twelve Boundaries.[53] They are the Four Sides of the World, with *three* each on each side. These *three* are *nine* on each side – *nine* on the east side, *nine* on the west side, *nine* on the north side, *nine* on the south side, plus the point which stands above them in the middle. Consequently, this point completes every side, since it stands in the middle: *ten* on the east side, *ten* on the west side, *ten* on the north side, *ten* on the south side – Ten Sephirot on every side. These are the Forty Letters that exist in the mystery of *In the beginning* below, in the mystery of the Holy Name, plus two Handles[54] for holding[55] the Left and the Right. These all exist in the mystery of *he*. Consequently *he* is found to [participate] in all these upper mysteries: the Holy Chariot, the *thirteen*,[56] the mystery of Ten Sephirot, the mystery of the Forty Two Engraved Letters that are in the Holy Name – for all [of them] are included in the image of *he*. They are all arranged diagonally, in the mystery of the point which stands in the

---

[51]ZHM adds here: *[each one of the Holy Names includes a Holy Chariot within it]*

[52]*letters* – in MS. O this word is missing

[53]*These Thirteen . . . Boundaries* – other texts read: *These twelve are the Twelve Boundaries.*

[54]*Handles* – ZHM has an alternative text which omits this word.

[55]*for holding* – other texts read: *to be unified with*

[56]*thirteen* – other texts read: *twelve*

middle and mediates between them all in a balanced fashion[57] – one side with another, and so on with respect to all four sides. They all exist in [the form of] a balance scale in equilibrium, which exists in order to establish everything.

[Creation of Lower Worlds with the Final Letter He: 143–158]

All these lower beings were created and established with this mystery. Concerning this it is written, "And God said, Let us make man is our image, after our likeness." (Gen.1.26) *Let us make* – this is *he* and all those which stand below, and are unified in its very image, in the fact that it is called *he*. (Aside from that which is unified above[58] in that which does not appear in its image at all and is not inscribed so that it be shown) when it is called *he*, it is filled with all these mysteries – it is everything. For this reason, that point stands in the middle, because it is unified with[59] everything:[60] it is unified with those which are on the eastern side, and it is with them.[61] For this reason, it is in all of them, and they are all in it, and all of them are *he*. Concerning this it is written, "Let us make man", and it is written, "And God said". Everything participates in the upper mystery as it should be. All these mysteries, and all the upper mysteries can be discerned in the [image of these] letters. They are inscribed in that very letter itself, so that the Holy Name may be unified as is truly fitting. This all is an upper mystery of the Holy Name. Up to here, upper wisdom concerning the mystery of the final letter

---

[57]*in a balanced fashion* – literally: *in a level path*

[58]*Aside from that which is unified above* – MS. O reads: *Aside from the "he", which is unified above* .... ZHV and ZHM read: *Aside from the fact that there in One above* ...

[59]*unified with* – or: *cleaves to*

[60]*everything* – ZC reads: *the heart*

[61]*it is unified ... with them* – later texts read: *those which are on the eastern side, it is unified with it, and it is with them*. ZHM adds here: *[those which are on the southern side, it is unified with it, and it is with them; it is unified with those which are on the northern side, and it is with them]*

## TRANSLATION

*he* of the four letters has been hinted at. Fortunate is he who enters and exits, and knows the ways of the Holy One, blessed be He, so that he may enter the World to Come without shame.

## [Letter Vav]

[Introduction to Letter Vav: 158–164]

The mystery of letter *vav* – a Holy Upper Chariot which stands[62] in the Fullness of Existence.[63] This letter divides into two letters which are two *vavs*, one *vav* just like the other[64] – they are twelve upper mysteries. This upper *vav* exists in five upper supports, over which the upper letter *he* stands. Even though this *vav* is *six* and the *mystery of six*, it is [also] *five* and the *mystery of five*, and all is as it should be.

## [The Right Side]

[The First Stage on the Right Side: 164–171]

The first phase on the right side – the mystery of the Primordial Light. It stands on a chariot which is [structured in] *sets of three*, not *four*. Even though every chariot must be four [sided],[65] everything here is in the mystery of *sets of three*, just like the letters of the Holy Name. For this reason, everything here proceeds in *sets of three*. Letter *he*[66] is the fourth letter – because of this, the chariot as a whole is [included] in the [mystery] of *four*.[67] Even though it is

---

[62] *stands* – or: *exists*

[63] *in the Fullness of Existence* – literally: *with a perfect (or complete) existence*

[64] *other* – ZC adds here: *[vav]*

[65] *every chariot must be four [sided]* – or: *nothing is [considered] a chariot unless it is in four*

[66] *Letter he* – other texts add: *[which we have mentioned]*

[67] *the chariot as a whole ... four* – other texts read: *its chariot is in four*

## LETTER VAV – RIGHT SIDE

[included] in [the mystery of] *four*, it is [also included] in [the mystery of] *sets of three*, and everything proceeds evenly,[68] so that each one should match the other, and [all should] be one.

[The Second Stage on the Right Side: 171–184]

The chariot of the South side, which is Right, [includes] three[69] which emerge out of the Lamp when a spirit[70] arises which blows with twelve spirits[71] of incense,[72] raising a fragrance, yet not raising it.[73] [This chariot] includes three colors. It shines with a brightness which is drawn within it.[74] One [color] glows with Fire, one glows with Water, and one glows with Air. This [spirit] differentiates and becomes three. [But] when this spirit differentiates and becomes three colors, they are not Fire, or Water, or Air. Rather, when this spirit differentiates, each one shines, and glows, and strengthens[75] the place which is above it. Afterwards it becomes a support below it. Within one color, the Fire which is included in the right side glows and becomes dominant. Within another color, the Water which is included in the right side glows and becomes dominant. Within another color, the Air which is included in the right side glows and becomes dominant. These three colors are one chariot for the right side in the mystery of letter *vav*.[76]

---

[68]*evenly* – literally: *in a level path*

[69]*[includes] three* – other texts read: *that chariot [includes] three*

[70]*spirit* – or: *breeze*

[71]*spirits* – or: *breezes*

[72]*twelve spirits of incense* – MS. S reads: *twelve fragrances of incense.* ZC reads: *twelve Boundaries.* ZHV reads: *twelve spirits*

[73]*raising a fragrance, yet not raising it* – ZHV reads: *raising fragrances, yet not raising them.* ZHM reads: *raising spirits (or breezes), yet not raising them*

[74]*which is drawn within it* – meaning of Aramaic uncertain

[75]*strengthens* – literally: *gives its force to*

[76]*letter vav* – later texts read: *letter he*

TRANSLATION

[The Names of the First Two Stages on the Right Side: 184–192]

These [colors] are *descriptive terms* which refer to the Holy One, blessed be He, in the mystery of the Names by which he is called. For this reason, the Holy One, blessed be He,[77] is called by many names, all of which are included in the various mysteries of the upper sides, which are the Names which it is forbidden to erase. This side, which is Right, is called *El*. Its chariot is called, in its totality, *Great*. When this chariot, which is these three colors, differentiates, they are the names which are called: [78] *Great, Strong,*[79] *Holy*. These are a chariot for the Right which is called *El*, an upper mystery, one of the Ten Names, as we have explained.

[The Third Stage on the Right Side: 192–195]

These three colors, which are a chariot for the right side, glow and shine,[80] and each one of these three colors differentiates into two others, to each side, until they arrive at the sum of *three times three*, which is *nine*, while the Right, which is above those which are ridden upon,[81] completes [the number] *ten*.

[The Names of the Third Stage on the Right Side: 196–204]

So also, these are called Upper and Lesser Sephirot – they are all attributes of the Holy One, blessed be He. The two which emerge from the color in which Water predominates: one is called *merciful* and the other is called *gracious*. These are from

---

[77] *the Holy One, blessed be He* – other texts read: *the Name of the Holy One, blessed be He*

[78] *they are the names which are called* – other texts read: *the resulting names are called*

[79] *Strong* – MS. O reads: *Kind*

[80] *shine* – other texts add here: *[downward]*

[81] *which is above those which are ridden upon* – later texts read: *which rides upon them.* See notes line 195

the color in which Water predominates. The two which emerge from the color in which Fire predominates: one is called *slow to anger* and the other is called *abounding in kindness*. These are from the color in which Fire predominates. The two which emerge from the color in which Air predominates: one is called *kind* and the other is called *forgiving*. In the mystery of the Book of Enoch, one is called *good* and the other is called *upright*, the sign for this being, "Good and upright is the Lord." (Ps.25.8)

[The Fourth Stage on the Right Side: 204–207]

From these [colors], lights differentiate downward. All of them are chariots, one for the other. [Though] they are all *external descriptive terms*, they nevertheless do not cleave to the [Holy Name] above like these.[82] [Yet] all of them are included in the right side, and they are all [considered] one with regard to this side. They are all in the mystery of letter *vav*.

**[The Left Side]**

[The First Stage on the Left Side: 207–211]

The first phase on the left side – the mystery of the Darkness which extends in darkness downward, until glowing Hell is created from that darkness of harsh, red-black fire. Here harsh flashes glow, which well up and are drawn downward. They all proceed from[83] the Darkness which is Left.

---

[82]*like these* – other texts read: *in these*
[83]*proceed from* – literally: *are out of*

TRANSLATION

[Transition to Stage Two on the Left Side: 211-215]

When[84] the Lamp arises out of the measuring of the Measuring Line, it shines to the right side.[85] From that shining, it shines to this side,[86] toward the Darkness – and lights approach this Fire. They draw the Fire closer to the Right,[87] and [the Darkness] is infused with its light.[88]

[Stage Two on the Left Side: 215-228]

Then, another spirit, which shines[89] (glowing), extends and shines out of the Lamp. This [spirit] extends in order to become a chariot for the left side. It extends, in the mystery of *three colors*, toward that side which is called North. But this spirit does not arise with incense or with fragrance, because it is the Left which rests upon this spirit which differentiates into three colors. These colors shine in the three sides of Fire, which is the left side: Fire the color of *darkness*, Fire the color of *red*, Fire the color of *black*. These three colors, which differentiate out of the spirit which emerges from the Lamp, support two sides. The first color,[90] Fire the color of *darkness* which is on the left side, glows and becomes dominant. Within the second color, Fire the color of *red* which is on the left side

---

[84]*When* – ZHV and ZHM read: – *except for*, or: *external to*

[85]*it shines to the right side* – ZHV and ZHM read: *that which shines from the right side*. According to the text as it stands the Lamp itself arises from the measuring of the Measuring Line. According to the reading in ZHV and ZHM *"that which shines from the right side"* arises from the measuring of the Measuring Line.

[86]*to this side* – These words have been moved here from the beginning of the previous sentence for the sake of clarity. ZHM reads these words as belonging to the end of the previous section.

[87]*They draw the Fire closer to the Right* – literally: *They draw close to that Fire, to that Right*

[88]*is infused with its light* – literally: *shines from it*

[89]*shines* – later texts read: *glows*

[90]*The first color* – later texts read: *Within the first color*

## LETTER VAV – LEFT SIDE

glows and becomes dominant. Within the third color, Fire the color of *black* which is on the left side glows and becomes dominant. These three colors are one chariot for the left side in the mystery of letter *vav*.

[The Names of the First Two Stages on the Left Side: 228-232]

These are called *descriptive terms* [which refer] to the Holy One, blessed be He, in the mystery of Left. One is called *Majestic*, one is called *Powerful*, and, in its totality, it is called *Mighty*, because this side is called Left – it is *Elohim*. We have explained that many sides are called *Elohim*.

[Stage Three on the Left Side: 232-236]

These three colors, which are on the left side, glow – they shine downward, and each one of these three colors differentiates into two others, to each side, until they arrive at the sum of *three times three*, which is *nine*, just as we explained on the other side, while the Left, which rides upon them, completes [the number] *ten*.

[The Names of the Third Stage on the Left Side: 236-242]

The two which emerge from the color which includes the color of *darkness*:[91] one is called *judge* and the other is called *magistrate*, as it is written, "For Elohim is a judge", (Ps.50.6) and it is written, "The father of orphans and the magistrate of widows is Elohim in his holy habitation." (Ps.68.6) The two which emerge from the color which is included within the Red Fire: one is called *mighty in strength* and the other is called *man of war*. The two which emerge from the color which is included and predominates within the Black Fire: one is called *visits iniquity* and the other is called *deals retribution*.

---

[91]*which includes the color of darkness* – reading *itpeal* as transitive. Other texts read: *which is included within Fire the color of darkness* – reading *itpeal* as passive.

TRANSLATION

[Stage Four on the Left Side: 242–249]

From here on, countless *mighty acts* differentiate downward,[92] all of which are *words*[93] on the left side, by which the Holy One, blessed be He, is called. They are all chariots below, to every side; but they are all in the mystery of the letter *vav* – because each of the four letters that are in the mystery of the Holy Name stands upon holy chariots, supports upon which they rest, and all [of these letters] are inscribed above [their chariots], each one as is appropriate for it. These chariots are *descriptive terms* which refer to the Name[94] to which they belong.[95]

[Conclusion of Left Side: 249–256]

For this reason, one who wishes[96] to unify the Holy Name must know to which [Name] each of these names, these *descriptive terms*, belongs: which Name rules over them – on the side to which each chariot belongs[97] – all in the mystery of the Holy Name, in these four letters by which the Holy One, blessed be He, is called. Fortunate are the Righteous who walk in the true path,[98] fortunate are they in This World, and

---

[92]*countless mighty acts differentiate downward* – ZHM reads: *many mighty acts differentiate downward, [all of which are from these three colors which we have mentioned – concerning this it is written, "Who can tell the mighty acts of YHVH . . . (Ps. 106.2)",] because they are countless* – adding the words between the brackets

[93]*words* – ZHM reads: *included*

[94]*Name* – other texts read: *Holy Name*

[95]*to which they belong* – literally: *with respect to which they stand*

[96]*one who wishes* – literally: *he who comes*

[97]*which Name rules over them – on the side to which each chariot belongs* – ZHM adds: *which Name rules over them, [for from here they differentiate downward until they reach the appointed powers which are chariots below. All of them are known in the mystery of the Name which rules over them] and by the side to which each chariot belongs.*

[98]*in the true path* – literally: *on a level path*

## LETTER VAV – LEFT SIDE

fortunate are they in the World to Come, for the Holy One, blessed be He, loves them.

### [The Middle Side]

### [The First Stage on the Middle Side: 256-262]

The first phase on the middle side is in the Eastern Gate, for the Eastern Gate stands in the middle. It takes two sides to join them together[99] with *beams* and *doors*, on both this side and the other. This Gate includes all those which we have mentioned, and it stands upon an upper chariot which belongs to the mystery of letter *vav*. This is *vav*, the totality of[100] them all. It exists in the mystery of all six upper sides.

### [Stage Two on the Middle Side: 262-273]

This [side] stands on a chariot which is three, including both Right and Left.[101] [It] emerges from the Lamp, when the spirit[102] arises which blows with twelve fragrances[103] of incense, raising fragrances – yet they do not rise.[104] This spirit shines with brilliance. It is the spirit which is *Whole*, and it is called *Peace*. When this spirit differentiates, it differentiates into three glowing colors: Fire,[105] Water, and Air,[106] just like[107] on the right side. But when it[108] differentiates, each one glows

---

[99] *to join them together* – literally: *to pass through them*

[100] *the totality of* – later texts read: *which includes*

[101] *including both Right and Left* – or: *in [the mystery of] Right and Left* – literally: *in Right and Left*

[102] *spirit* – or: *breeze*. Later texts read: *vav*

[103] *fragrances* – other texts read: *spirits (breezes)*

[104] *yet they do not rise* – ZHM reads: *yet not raising them*

[105] *glowing colors: Fire ...* – other texts read: *colors, glowing with Fire ...*

[106] *Water and Air* – later texts read: *Air and Water*

[107] *just like* – other texts: *as it was explained*

[108] *But when it* – i.e. the middle side, in contradistinction to the right side

in its *own* place, and the brilliance, which extends from this spirit, strengthens *each* of these three sides. The first color glows with Fire and it strengthens it. The second color glows with Water and it increases it. The third color glows with Air and it infuses it with a light, like purple – glowing with these two sides. These three colors are one chariot in the mystery of letter *vav*, and it is the mystery of letter *vav*.

[The Names of the First Two Stages on the Middle Side: 273-285]

These [colors] are *descriptive terms* by which the Holy One, blessed be He, is called – as has already been explained – for the Holy One, blessed be He, is called by all these names. These *descriptive terms* are included in the mystery of the Holy Name by which this middle side[109] is called. Even though this [side] is called by letter *vav*,[110] it subsumes[111] all the names, upper and lower – all four letters of the Holy Name are unified in it, because it subsumes all sides, above and below. This is the mystery of *YHV*. This name belongs here, and it is *YHVH*. It takes two letters above and one below, and it stands in the middle, between above and below, and [between] the two sides as we have said. Its chariot is called *Awesome* in its totality. When this chariot, which is the spirit that we have mentioned, differentiates into three other colors, which are called *Awesome, Faithful, Extends Kindness*,[112] these three three constitute the Holy Chariot for the side which stands in the middle.

---

[109]*side* – later texts read: *name*

[110]*by letter vav* – other texts read: *in the mystery of letter vav*

[111]*subsumes* – literally: *takes*

[112]*Faithful, Extends Kindness* – MS. O reads: *Extends Kindness, Faithful*

## LETTER VAV – THE MIDDLE SIDE

[Stage Three on the Middle Side: 285–295]

These three colors, which are a Holy Chariot for letter *vav*, glow and shine downward, and each one of the three colors differentiates into two others, to each side, until they become the sum of *three times three* to each side, which is *nine*, while the Holy Name which rules over them completes [the number] *ten*. Each one of the three sides which we have mentioned, Right, Left, and Middle, each one in the mystery of its chariots, is *ten*, because everything, above and below, is together in a state of perfection.[113] They are the Ten Sephirot, the Ten Utterances – and all of their chariots, in the side which rules over them, are called Ten Sephirot, Ten Utterances.[114] For this reason, each one of these sides reaches *ten*, and from there, to a vast number – because the chariots differentiate to each side, until each one reaches a vast number.[115]

[The Names of the Third Stage on the Middle Side: 295–307]

Come and see: All of these chariots, when they differentiate to their [various] sides, are called by the name which rules over them, in the mystery of that very letter itself below. The two which emerge from one point: one is called *forgives iniquity* and the other is called *remits transgression*. These are[116] from the color in which Water predominates. The two which emerge from the color in which Fire predominates: one is called *lofty* and the other is called *high*. In the mystery of Enoch these names are included in the World to Come,

---

[113] *together in a state of perfection* – literally: *in a single perfectedness*

[114] *and all of their chariots ... Ten Utterances* – this passage is missing in MS. O

[115] *For this reason, each one ... a vast number.* – later texts have a shortened version of this passage: *For this reason, each one of these sides reaches ten chariots to each side, until each one reaches a vast number.*

[116] *are* – MS. O reads: *letters are*

whereas here, on this side, [their place is taken by] *tests the heart. Lofty* as it is written, "Your judgements are too lofty for him", (Ps.10.5) and it is written, "*YHVH* is majestic in loftiness." (Ps.93.4) Even though this name belongs to the World to Come, nevertheless *lofty* is written. For this reason, the World to Come participates in all these [names], and thus it is called *Elohim* just like[117] the Left, and all is one. The two which emerge from the third color, in which Air predominates: one is called[118] *dwells forever* and the other is called *holy*.

[Stage Four on the Middle Side: 307–310]

From these [colors], lights differentiate downward, and all of them are chariots, one for the other. All of them are *descriptive terms* by which the Holy One, blessed be He, is called – they can all be recognized [as belonging to] the side[119] which rules over them.

[The Three Lower Sides: 310–322]

In a like manner, there are three sides which emerge from these upper sides which we have mentioned, which are Right, Left, and Middle. These extend further out than these – two of them extend.[120] All of them take chariots below, just like these upper [sides], but they are not upper [sides] in comparison to them. These lower [sides] which emerge from these upper sides, which we have mentioned, are precisely comparable to them – one is called Right, one is called Left, and one which stands in the middle within that Middle which we have mentioned. All of them are included in these three

---

[117] *just like* – MS. S and ZC read: *in the colors of*. ZHV and ZHM read: *like the colors of*

[118] *The two which emerge . . . is called . . .* – later texts read: *Air predominates in the third color. The two which emerge from it: one is called . . .*

[119] *they can . . . the side* – literally: *they are all known in the side*

[120] *two of them extend* – other texts read: *two of them stand outside*

## LETTER VAV – THE THREE LOWER SIDES

upper [sides], and all of them are included in[121] the mystery of the letter *vav*, which includes all of them. They all have specific chariots[122] which differentiate to their [various] sides. These [chariots] are not called by specific names, but rather by *lower descriptive terms*, which are comparable to the *upper descriptive terms*. [Though] those below are unified with those above, these three other [sides] are all *external* chariots. This has been explained.

[The Names of the Three Lower Sides: 322–334]

Come and see: These two beings are external supports. They are Right and Left, and are called *the Kindnesses of David*. They are *Tsvaot*. Their chariot consists of two that stand ready to carry out [their] agency with regard to the true prophets. From there, *deeds* differentiate outward into the revealed world.[123] This is the mystery of the verse, "Great are the acts of *YHVH*" (Ps.111.2) – *great [deeds]* which emerge from *Great*. These are called "your great mercies, *YHVH*," (Ps.119.156) "Where are your kindnesses, etc.," (Ps.89.50) "Remember your mercies, *YHVH*, and your kindnesses, for they are forever." (Ps.25.6) Even though we have explained that they are above,[124] they are *forever* below. For this reason

---

[121]*in these three upper [sides], and all of them are included in* – This passage is missing in MS. O.

[122]*They all have specific chariots* – literally: *They are all in known chariots*

[123]*outward into the revealed world* – literally: *in the world to be revealed.* Later texts read: *in the world openly*

[124]ZHM adds here: *[nevertheless they differentiate downward in the manner of above, as it is written, "for they are forever"* – *they are forever above,]*

## TRANSLATION

they are not called by names in the way in which those which are above are called by names. While they are exactly comparable to those which are above, they are [nevertheless] included in those which exist outside. They are the supports of the Torah which emerge from the upper chariots. It was these, and this is it which King David mentioned constantly,[125] in its totality,[126] as we have explained.

---

[125] *It was these ... mentioned constantly* – ZHM reads: *It was these which King David mentioned, and this which he mentioned constantly*

[126] *in its totality* – or: *generally*

## Critical and Explanatory Notes to the Translation

The translation as a rule follows MS. O, unless otherwise noted. All items in the translation found in square brackets [ ], whether headings, line numbers, or brief explanatory phrases, are the additions of the translator. Likewise, all verse references have been added by the translator, though fairly complete and accurate references are to be found in ZC. Any words or phrases included in the translation which have been added from others sources are marked only by a numbered footnote, which gives the reading in MS. O.

Abbreviations used in footnotes to the translation:

> MS. O = Oxford Manuscript / MS. S = Jewish Theological Seminary Manuscript / ZC = Zohar Cremona / ZHS = Zohar Hadash Salonika / ZHV = Zohar Hadash Venice / ZHM = Zohar Hadash Munkatch / *Ketem Paz* = textual emendations of Rabbi Shimon Lavi. For more details see the introduction to the Aramaic text.

> *other texts* = MS. S and/or ZC; translation follows MS.O / *later texts* = ZHV and ZHM; translation follows MSS. and ZC / *early texts* = MSS. and ZC; translation follows ZHV and ZHM. For more detailed information see the critical apparatus of the Aramaic text.

The footnotes to the translation have been limited to points of text and translation only. The following critical and explanatory notes attempt to clarify a few of the many textual and terminological obscurities which our text presents.

Line 1(1): *The Secrets of the Letters of the Divine Name from the Zohar*

> The title is written in Hebrew, not in Aramaic. It is lacking entirely in both ZC and MS. S. In ZHS, the editors report that they were informed that the passage was titled as above, but do not themselves seem to have possessed any text which bore a title.

> In MS. O, the words *"of the Divine Name"* are abbreviated השי"ת. In ZHS this was shortened to הש"י. This was misinterpreted by the printers of ZHV as an abbreviation for השייכים, *which belong to*. The resulting title was: *THE SECRETS OF THE LETTERS which belong to the Zohar*. Since this last part of the title was now trivial (all texts in the Zohar belong to the Zohar!), it was omitted, leaving the apocopated title: *THE SECRETS OF THE LETTERS*.

> ZHS contained a clear designation of the end of our text. This designation was omitted in ZHV and in subsequent editions. This led later printers to apply the now apocopated title to an entire string of unrelated texts, blurring the precise parameters, content, and structure of our text. Thus Scholem

## NOTES TO TRANSLATION

(*Major Trends* p. 162, letter *p*) includes this entire group of unrelated texts under the title *Secrets of the Letters*. This error was noted and corrected by Tishbi, *Mishnat HaZohar* vol. 1 p.21 note 3.

Line 1(2): *Who can tell, etc.*

For the use of this verse as an introduction to the description of God's creation, see *Pirke Rabbi Eliezer*, the beginning of ch.3. In the Zohar, *mighty acts* have a more specific and technical sense, referring to the progressive emergence of the forces of Judgement. For this, see the long text (ZHM) to lines 242–243 in the footnotes to the translation.

Line 4: *Impression of Existence (Permanence)*

סרטא דקיומא: This is the reading in the MSS., ZC, the *Ketem Paz*, and the *Ramaz* (*Hadrat Melech* 105a, reprint Bnei Brak 1974.) ZHV has the reading סטרא, *side*, a much more common word in the Zohar. Most subsequent editions follow ZHV, or include both readings.

The *Ketem Paz* interprets the term סרטא = רושם, *impression/mark*, basing himself on Mishna Shabbat 12:4. In Tosephta Shabbat 11:6 (ed. Lieberman, New York 1962 p.47) this precise form of the word is used. This text is concerned with the prohibition of *writing* on Shabbat, whether in order to be liable for punishment one must write an intelligible letter, taken from some alphabet, or whether any *mark* is equally prohibited. סרטא is therefore a form of writing which precedes the specificity of *letters*, a sense which fits the context here perfectly.

This rabbinic source enlightens another aspect of this obscure phrase. In order for writing to be included in the prohibition on Shabbat it must be *permanent* – something which is מתקיים. קיום in this context therefore carries the double sense of a permanent impression made on some medium, as well as the regular medieval philosophical sense of existence. For a full discussion of this term see Liebes, *Chapters*, especially p.355 §1 and p.356 §4.

This analysis yields a paradoxical reading of the phrase: it is only an *impression*, not yet articulate and definite; nevertheless it has *permanence* and *existence*. Similarly, the reading in MS. S and ZC to line 4, *inscribed letters*, has a paradoxical sense: they are *letters*, hence articulate and definite, but only *inscribed* (רושם), neither articulate nor definite.

Line 8: *Mystery*

*Raza* (רזא) – mystery – is the Aramaic translation of the Hebrew word *Sod* (סוד). *Sod* in turn has an affinity, both phonetic and semantic, with the term *Yesod* (יסוד), *fundamental truth* or *principle*. (Cf. Jastrow p. 961.) In the Zohar

## NOTES TO TRANSLATION

it carries a sense of *formal participation* – the essential similarity of one entity to another. A certain truth can be the *Raza* of a verse, whose words represent or correspond to that truth (SLDN ll.32–42). Alternatively, if one being shares the notion of *threeness*, it will then be *in the Raza of Three* (SLDN ll.158–171).

A relatively clear example can be found in the following passage (Zohar vol. 2 135a): "Just as they are unified above in *One*, so also it is unified below in the mystery of One, in order to be with them above, One corresponding to One." God is One. His Throne *participates* in this Oneness. Therefore the Throne is *in the mystery of One*, while God himself is *in One*. Similarly, in line 297 below, the chariots which emerge from a given *side* are *in the mystery of that side below*.

A source for this usage can be found in the *Book of Creation*, where the term *Yesod* (יסוד) is employed throughout to designate archetypal parallel phenomena in the cosmic order. These elements of *participation* and *parallelism* are essential to the Zohar's notion of *Raza* – *mystery*. Consequently, the first two lines of our passage here distinguish two levels: *letter yod* on the one hand, and the *mystery of letter yod* on the other. The relation between them is designated by the words *corresponding to this*.

Line 9(1): *Crowns*

*Its Crowns* – עטרוי from the root עטר. This root has three primary meanings: 1) to be crowned, literally; 2) to be adorned and beautified, as a crown adorns the head; 3) to be distinguished, in the sense of displaying and manifesting one's beauty. (Cf. Jastrow p.1064.)

In our text the term is used for the branching out and interlocking of a given hypostasis with those which exist both above and below it. Here in line 9, I translated the noun form literally, since Hebrew letters have crowns on top of them (though *yod* has only a single tip which points up). In line 52, I translated the verbal form as *to be made manifest*, since the context indicates that the sense is the *showing* of the beauty which is hidden above. In line 59, I translated the verbal form as *to be adorned*, as the primary extension of the literal meaning, since the motion upward could not be construed as a *manifestation* of beauty.

Line 9(2): *One Hundred Worlds*

*One Hundred Worlds*, מאה עלמין, is an unusual phrase whose symbolic reference is uncertain. The reading is confirmed by the MSS., ZC, the *Ketem Paz* and the *Ramaz*. In ZHS an "alternative reading" is brought: מארי instead of מאה. This is a doubtful reading, as it may only reflect the printer's inability to distinguish a ה from a ר with a י written within it, a common orthographic practice in many Zohar manuscripts. In ZHV the word מאה is omitted altogether. Based on this faulty text, the Vilna Gaon (commentary to Tikkune ZH 23a/80b) emends עלמין, *worlds*, changing it to עלאין, *upper beings*.

It seems fairly certain that *One Hundred Worlds* is an alternative form of the phrase *One Thousand Worlds*. These are the *One Thousand Worlds* which existed before the creation of the world (ZHM 5a). They reflect the stage of creation before the emergence of the Divine Name (ibid), a stage of pure Will and undifferentiated Thought – before the emergence of definite and knowable Wisdom which is represented by the Letters of the Divine Name.

The connection is made by means of the simple mathematical "equation": $1 = 10 = 100 = 1000$, which is mentioned in SLDN ll.511–512, as well as in *Shaare Orah* p.60.

Lines 11–13: *Below it / Nut*

See the readings of *Ketem Paz* in footnotes 8–9 to the translation. In both these cases the relation of the letter *yod* and the Nut is reversed – instead of the Nut standing below letter *yod*, and serving as its chariot, it is letter *yod* which stands below the Nut and serves as *its* chariot.

The term *Nut* here seems to have presented some problem for interpreters of the Zohar. Its usual symbolic references (M. Cordovero, *Pardes Rimmonim* vol. 2 1d) do not seem to fit the context. The editors of ZHM possessed a copy of the Amsterdam edition of ZH with texual emendations written in the margin. These emendations replace every instance of the term Nut with the term Point. Cf. Liebes, *Chapters* p.21 §6 and p.22 §12.

I suspect that the term *Nut* does not have any fixed symbolic reference in our text, but rather refers to a certain notion which views reality as an infinite chain of "Chinese Boxes," one inside the other, where each link in the chain is considered an *external shell* with respect to that which is above it, and at the same time an *internal kernel* with respect to that which is below it. See below lines 339–347 and Zohar vol. 1 19b–20a. For the source of this model see J. Schlanger, *The Philosophy of Solomon Ibn Gabirol* (Jerusalem 1979) pp. 73–74.

Lines 15–31: *Measuring Line, Points, Knots*

Parallel passages which use language and symbols similar to those employed in this passage can be found in ZHM 81b and ZHM 93a–96a.

## NOTES TO TRANSLATION

Line 19(1): *Lamp*

For a full analysis of this term in the Zohar see Liebes, *Chapters*, pp.136–167.

Line 19(2): *First Tip/Knot*

The reading *first knot* is supported by the parallel constructions *second knot* (line 23) and *third knot* (line 26). The reading *first* (=upper) *tip* is supported by the parallel construction *lower tip* (line 22). There is no substantial difference in meaning between the two readings. According to Zohar vol. 3 10b, the *letter yod* is divided into three parts, each of which is designated by the term *knot*. These three parts are identified with the *upper tip*, the *lower tip* and the *main body* of the letter yod. Cf. Liebes, *Chapters* p.397 §11.

Line 27: *Sand, The Profane*

חול – See the passage from ZHM 21b cited in §14 above.

Line 33: *The Infinite*

The term אין סוף, *The Infinite*, is in all later Kabbalistic systems a term for the transcendent Creator. Here, and even more clearly below in line 43, it seems that this term does *not* refer to the Transcendent Creator. He is designated by phrases like *the One who strikes, He who is not known*. It is He who causes the אין סוף to shine (line 43). From this it seems clear that they are distinct entities. אין סוף seems to refer to some aspect of God's Will or His Thought. See also SLDN 11.345 and 616, and cf. Zohar vol. 1 15a, which is a parallel text to our text.

Even though the Zohar may not apply this *term* to the Creator, it is nevertheless perfectly clear that the Zohar holds that there *is* a Transcendent Creator (§13 above). Cf. Ben Shlomo's introduction to *Shaare Orah* pp. 30–31.

Line 37: *Moses*

Moses is identified with letter *vav*. Therefore he cannot grasp the secrets of letter *yod* which transcend his level. See Zohar volume 1 21b, for the identification of various prophets with different aspects of letter *vav*.

Line 46: *like ... into a palace*

See Zohar vol. 2 99a for the parable of the *palace*.

## NOTES TO TRANSLATION

Line 54: *wonders*

נפלאות - This word breaks up into נ = 50 and פלאות = *which are beyond understanding*. Cf. the Aramaic Targum to Deut. 17.8.

Line 70: *four directions of the world*

North, South, and East are identified with the three sides of letter *vav*, while West is identified with *final letter he*. See also Zohar vol. 2 24a.

Line 89: *Michael, Gabriel, Rafael, Uriel*

See *Pirke Rabbi Eliezer* ch.4 (ed. D. Luria 9b) and Midrash Numbers Rabbah 2:10.

Lines 91-92: *he [originally] was dalet*

See Zohar vol. 2 123b and 178b.

Line 93: *The Mystery of Enoch*

Enoch (Gen.5.21-24) became an important figure in Jewish apocalyptic and mystical literature. The Targum Pseudo-Jonathan to Gen.5.24 relates how Enoch was raised up to the heavens by the word of God, and became *Metatron, the Great Scribe*. Continuing this tradition, the Zohar relates many different and contradictory legends concerning Enoch. See Zohar vol. 1 21a and 56b.

There are two elements of these Enoch traditions which particularly concern our text. In vol. 2 277 we are told that Enoch came into possession of a book of ancient hidden wisdom - this is presumably the *mystery of the book of Enoch* mentioned in line 203 below. It may also be the *mystery of Enoch* mentioned here and in line 301. However another mystery concerning Enoch is related in this passage which ties the person of Enoch himself to the execution of *harsh judgement* in this world. It is more likely that this is the meaning of of *the mystery of Enoch* here in line 93.

Line 98: *permission*

Cf. MRI p.38 and §4 above.

Lines 102-103: *Wherever you find Michael... the Indwelling*

See Midrash Exodus Rabbah 2:5.

## NOTES TO TRANSLATION

Line 105: *approach it*

The translation follows the reading (ZHV and ZHM) קדמה לה, where the word קדמה is a verb. In the MSS. and ZC the reading is קדמאה לה, which yields the translation: *and the first letter yod is for it*. Aside from the grammatical difficulties (which one must get used to in translating the Zohar), the terms *first letter yod* or *first letter aleph* do not seem to have much meaning, since, unlike letter he (*first letter he / final letter he*), these letters have no lower counterparts in SLDN such that the upper one could be called *first*. But see Zohar vol. 2 177a.

Line 107: *passes away, is broken*

The word אתברת could come either from the root תבר (to break) or from the root עבר (to pass) with the assimilation of the first letter ע. MS. S has the full form אתעברת.

Line 109: *in the Name with respect to which it forms a support*

The simplified rendering, included in translation, was based on reading אסתמיך as a reflexive, not as a passive, and understanding על מה in the sense of *"with respect to which,"* not in its simple meaning *"upon which."* The former reading is supported by lines 19–27, where the verb אסתמיך is used with the preposition *below*. The latter reading finds some support in line 249 where על מה means *"with respect to which."*

Nevertheless, the convoluted translation, placed in the footnote, seems more faithful to the original. It is based on breaking the word שמא from the phrase על מה דאסתמיך, reading the former as standing in apposition to the words *"that letter"* (emphasizing the identification of letters and Names), and the latter as referring back to the words *"its chariot."* The two phrases: *In that letter / its chariot // In that Name / upon which it rests* – form a kind of parallelism. This reading is consonant with both the kind of involuted thought patterns which come up repeatedly in SLDN, and with the poetic approach to the language of the Zohar which Dr. Daniel Matt has emphasized in his new translation of selected passages from Zohar.

Lines 115–119 *But [you might object that] all* ...

Only MS. O has the text included in the translation, while all the other texts have the reading which has been placed in the footnote. *Prima facia* this latter reading has the following advantages:

1) The second sentence (*But all* . . . ) is a simple declarative sentence whose content follows directly from the content of the first sentence. On

## NOTES TO TRANSLATION

the other hand, the reading in MS. O, if read as a declarative sentence, *contradicts* the previous sentence.

2) The reading *"chariots which are not external,"* which is parallel to the uncontested reading *"included in the external lower [powers],"* seems superior to the reading *"chariots which are not [accessible] to all,"* which comes out of the blue and has internal difficulties.

Nevertheless, the objections which can be raised against this text are much stronger:

1) There is no reason for the second sentence to begin with the word *"but."* Since there is no tension or opposition between the sentences at all, *"and"* would be more appropriate.

2) The reading *"Only this one, because this letter is included in the external [powers]"* contains certain problems. The opening phrase, *"Only this one,"* asserts that the letter *he* is different from the other three letters of the Name – but with respect to what? One possibility is that *only this one* is included in the lower powers. What is the reason for this distinction? The text goes on to explain that this is because letter *he* is included in the external powers. This yields the tautology: letter *he* is included in the lower powers because letter *he* is included in the lower powers.

The other possibility is that letter *he* is distinguished from the other letters in that it is revealed. The text would then be saying that letter *he* is revealed because it is included in the lower powers. This would not be a tautology, but it would contradict the previous sentence which asserted the exact opposite: that letter *he* is included in the lower powers *because it is revealed*. The easier reading *linguistically*, is more difficult as regards *the content*.

3) The final words of this reading, *"which are not external,"* when connected to the next sentence, *"except when the palaces join together,"* yields the following inference: When the palaces join together, the upper Holy Chariots become lower external chariots! It is more plausible to posit that through this process of mediation they become *"accessible to all."* Again, the more difficult linguistic reading of MS. O reflects more careful attention to the flow of the argument.

Regarding the relation of the opening sentences to each other, it seems more likely that this passage reflects the casuistic style of the Talmud. While accepting the reading of MS. O, I have not translated the second sentence of this passage as a declarative sentence which would contradict the opening sentence. Rather I have translated it as anticipating a possible question, in true Talmudic style, and as introducing the elaborate refutation of this

## NOTES TO TRANSLATION

hypothetical objection. For explicit examples of this kind of structure in SLDN, see ll.335–336 and 1.487 ff.

Lines 118–119: *when the palaces join together, etc.*

See Zohar vol. 1 41a–45b and vol.2 244b–262b.

Lines 124–142: [The Secrets Included in Final Letter He]

*thirteen attributes of mercy* – cf. Exodus 34:6–7 and Babylonian Talmud Rosh Hashanah 17b
*Twelve Boundaries* – cf. the Book of Creation ch.5:1
*Four Sides ... with three on each side* – Midrash Numbers Rabbah 2:10 states that the four angels which surround God's throne correspond both to the four sides of the world (NSEW) and to the tribes of Israel as they encamped in the desert (Num.2) – *three tribes* to each of the *four sides* of the world.
*nine on each side* – cf. *Sefer HaBahir* §95 (p.35) and SLDN ll.192–195.
*point ... in the middle* – cf. *Pirke Rabbi Eliezer* ch.4 (ed. D. Luria 9b).
*Ten Sephirot* – cf. the *Book of Creation* ch.1 and notes to 1.196.
*Forty Two Engraved Letters* – cf. Babylonian Talmud Kiddushin 71a.
*arranged diagonally* – cf. the *Book of Creation* ch.5:1.
*mediates* – אכרע; cf. the *Book of Creation* ch.3:1.
*balance scale* – cf. the *Book of Creation* ch.3:1 and §21 above.

Line 131: *this point completes*

MS. O has אשתלים, the reflexive form. MS. S and ZC have אשלים, the transitive form. This latter reading would seem superior, but, as Kadari has pointed out (*Grammar* p. 79), the Zohar regularly uses the *itpeal* in a transitive sense. Concerning his claim that the *itpeal* has lost its reflexive sense in the Zohar, see notes to line 109 above.

Line 135: *two handles for holding*

אזנין could mean either *handles* or *ears*. In either case, it is a symbol deriving from some concrete image which is alien to the immediate context. In the former case, it would seem to be the image of a vessel, in the latter some anthropomorphic image. The verb לאחדא could mean *to grasp hold of* or *to unify*. The reflexive form, cited in the footnotes to the text, clearly means *to be unified*. The transitive form in MS. O combines with אזנין to form the image of a vessel with two handles, which can be held on its left and right sides. The image, whatever it may be, is certainly unclear and out of its natural context. The text in ZHM eliminates the image altogether.

## NOTES TO TRANSLATION

Lines 152–153: *Let us make man / And God said*

This theme, which is referred to here only in passing, is developed at great length in ZHM4d ff. The notion that the world was created with the final letter *he* of God's Name is derived from the verse, "Who is like You, YHVH, among the powers (אלים)." (Ex.15.11) This verse is interpreted to mean that YHVH took the final letter *he* (ה) from his Name, and placed it in the middle of the four powers (the four letters אלים). In this way אלים (the four powers) became אלהים – *God* – who created the world.

Line 159: *The Fullness of Existence*

See Liebes, *Chapters* p.368 §53.

Line 190: *Strong, Kind*

The reading *Kind* (חסיד) is attested only in MS. O. It is the only element in the entire list of attributes which deviates from the otherwise identical list of attributes as found in *Shaare Orah* pp. 220–221 and p. 243. For the historical relations between these texts, see E. Gottlieb, *Studies*, Tel Aviv 1976, pp. 97–98.

Whether this reading derives from the author's own hand or from a scribal emendation, it is difficult to dismiss it as a mere copyist's error. This is not only because of the general reliability of MS. O, but also because of the *strategic location* of this one deviation within the standard list, a deviation which drawns our attention to the internal organization of the list.

In *Shaare Orah*, the term *Strong* stands above the two terms *slow to anger* and *abounding in kindness*. In SLDN these are the two which *emerge from the color in which fire predominates* (ll.199–200). This means that either *Strong* or *Kind* must be identified with *the color in which fire predominates*. Prima facia, the reading *Strong* (חסין) would seem to be the more likely candidate, since it is the only term on the right side with connotations of the strength and power which are characteristic of the left side of Judgement. But it is precisely its clear identification with the left side which makes its presence on the right problematic.

This point highlights one of the main differences between the Zohar's presentation of the attributes and Gikatilia's. Both Gikatilia and the Zohar use Aristotelean *language* to describe the interpenetration of the spiritual elements. But Gikatilia seems to understand this interpenetration as a matter of quantity and proportion in line with the Aristotelian notion of the four elements. According to Aristotle, every physical body contains all four elements, while the visible *qualitative* distinctions between different bodies reflect only the *quantitative* difference of varying proportions of the different elements within the admixture (§23 above). So also for Gikatilia, the Right is Water, despite the fact that it possesses a moderate amount of Air, and a small amount of Fire, because Water constitutes the *majority* of the admixture – it predominates (cf. p.243 bottom). For Gikatilia, who seems to assert the actual presence of an admixture of Judgement on the right side, the term *Strong*, which is an aspect of *power* and *might*, characteristic of Judgement, is appropriate.

But the Zohar explicitly rejects this understanding of the elements. He rejects any notion that the elements Air and Fire could be included on the Right (ll. 176–177). For the Zohar, a term like *Strong* would be wholly inappropriate on the Right. The reading *Kind*, even for an element which corresponds to the *fire which is included on the right*, fits well with the Zohar's understanding of the process described here – the *dialectical suppression of any expression of Judgement*. See also the notes to ll.220–222 below.

Line 191: *The Ten Names*

For the various opinions concerning the number of the Holy Names which may not be erased, see *Mishneh Torah*, Foundations 6.1–5, and the notes of Rabbi Jacob Cohen's there. Rabbi R. Margaliot (his edition of Zohar Hadash 2c note 15) cites the Midrash *The Fathers according to Rabbi Nathan* as the Zohar's source for the number ten. See also *Ketem Paz* vol. 1 p. 269a and *Shekel HaKodesh* pp. 125–130..

Line 195: *which is above those which are ridden upon*

דעלייהו דרכיבי – The word רכיבי is a plural passive participle. With the prefix ד, it yields: *which are ridden upon*. The alternative reading is דעלייהו רכיב – where רכיב is a singular active participle. Without the prefix it means: *he who rides*; plus דעלייהו, which means *which is upon them*, it yields: *he who rides upon them*.

This simpler reading, which is identical to the undisputed reading in l.235 (the left side), appears only in the later printed editions, and may be the result of the harmonization of l.195 with l.235. The more difficult earlier reading is present in all three early texts, MSS. O and S, and ZC. For this reason alone it is difficult to dismiss it as an error. Moreover, it is difficult to understand how such a strange and awkward form could arise through a copyist's error.

An explanation for this odd reading may be found in the very similarity between lines 195 and 235. The left and the right sides are parallel in structure. Their chariots take the first stages of pure dark and pure light from their unformed beginnings through several steps toward the eventual goal of stable and finite form. While their chariots are parallel in structure, their relative starting points are radically different: the primal light is above, while the burning fires of Gehinnom are below.

Therefore, though the notion of chariot, in the abstract sense of *agency* and *expression of creative potential* (§19 above), is appropriate for both the right and the left, the concrete image of chariot (where the rider rides *above* his chariot) is appropriate for the right only, but inappropriate for the left.

This visual distinction between the right and the left may also be found in the "topology" of the list of attributes. Comparing the three sides, there is a fundamental difference between the right and the middle, on the one hand, and the left, on the other. Of the three first attributes mentioned on each side, one is singled out as the "totality" of that chariot (lines 184-192, 228-232, 273-285). This general attribute is mentioned *first* in the Zohar text and appears at the *top* of Gikatilia's lists – on the right and the middle. On the left, it is mentioned *last* in the Zohar text, and in Gikatilia's lists it appears at the *bottom*. Since the Left alone is pictured as being *below* its chariot, its general attribute is pictured as gravitating toward the bottom of the list, because of its affinity to the Left, which is below.

This tension between the abstract and concrete senses of the *chariot* symbol is worth discussing in its own right. It may also provide a plausible motivation for twisting the phrasing of the right side, in order to distinguish it from the left. The reading דעלייהו דרכיבי for the right emphasizes the *presence* of the Holy Name *El above* its chariot. It may be intended to *contrast* with the reading דעלייהו רכיב on the left, where the notion רכיב has only its abstract meaning of *agency*, without any concrete sense of *presence above*.

Line 196: *Upper and Lesser Sephirot*

The term *ten sephirot* is first used in our text in ll.133 and 138, above. In l.292 below, the phrase *ten sephirot* is applied to the chariots of all three sides. (Or to both the Holy Names and their chariots according to the long text there.) Here, the phrase *sephirot* is also linked to the number *ten*. The only other place in the Zohar where the term *sephirot* is used (ZHM 3d-4d), it is in the context of the phrase *ten sephirot b'limah*, which is clearly drawn directly from the *Book of Creation* ch. 1. For use of this term in the Zohar, see *Major Trends*, p. 165, and Gottlieb, *Studies*, p.172.

The meaning of this term is unclear in the other passages cited. Here, however, it is unequivocally linked to two notions of the number *ten:* a) the ten names which it is forbidden to erase, and b) the *descriptive terms* which form groups of ten *(three times three* plus the Holy Name = 10). This seems to be the meaning of the relatively obscure phrase: *Upper and Lesser Sephirot* – the ten Holy Names which it is forbidden to erase are the Upper Sephirot, while the groups of ten *descriptive terms* are the Lesser Sephirot.

## NOTES TO TRANSLATION

The Zohar's use of the term *sephirot* is similar to that of his contemporary Joseph Gikatilia in that it refers to the Holy Names which may not be erased. However it differs in one major respect: the Zohar uses the phrase *sephirot* only in combination with the number *ten*, under the direct influence of the *Book of Creation*. For the Zohar the term *sephirot* (plural – never *sephirah* singular; see ZHM 3d–4d where the singular is ספר not ספירה!) refers to an abstract quality which a) cannot be separated from the number ten, and b) may be applied to entities other than the Ten Holy Names, which participate in the mystery of the *number ten*. It is not applied to the Holy Names as individuals, as a synonym for *name*, or *level*, or *side*, but only to all ten in their totality. Thus neither letter *he* nor letter *vav* is called *a sephirah*. Rather they each *participate* in the *mystery of ten sephirot*.

Scholem (*Major Trends* p.165) speculates that the Zohar is careful to avoid "modern sounding" expressions, and so refrains generally from using the term *sephirot*. This explanation seems unlikely, given the fact that the term *sephirot* derives from the *Book of Creation*, the oldest extant text of Jewish speculation. Scholem himself suggested (cf. *T'mirin 2*, Jerusalem 1981, p. 44) that the *Book of Creation* might derive from the Tannaitic period (second century C. E. – the time of Shimon bar Yohai, the traditional author of the Zohar!) Traditional opinion concerning the dating of the book was divided (cf. M. Cordovero, *Pardes Rimmonim*, Gate 1 ch. 1), but no one dated it later than the second century. If the author was concerned to pass his work off as a product of the second century, he could not have hurt his chances by using terminology which was generally assumed to derive from that period.

Lines 220–222: *the three sides of Fire ... Fire the color of darkness, Fire the color of red, Fire the color of black*

> See notes to 1.190. Here on the left side, the Zohar seems to be categorically rejecting the literal sense of the *element symbolism*, just as he did on the right side above. Gikatilia (*Shaare Orah* p. 243) describes the left side as an admixture in which a majority of Fire predominates, yet which also contains a small amount of Water and a moderate amount of Air. In contrast to this approach, the Zohar describes the left side as consisting of *three types of fire!* This would seem to support the interpretation of the *dialectical suppression* of the expression of Mercy on the left, just as Judgement was suppressed on the Right.

Lines 222–223: *These three colors, which differentiate out of the spirit which emerges from the Lamp, support two sides.*

> The precise meaning of these *two sides* is unclear. However, the development of these three colors, as described here, is very similar (though not identical) to the development of the *Dargin* of the *Sitra Achra* (Zohar vol. 2 242b–244b). If these parallel structures are meant to refer to the same entities, then the

## NOTES TO TRANSLATION

meaning of *two sides* would be the *Side of Holiness* and the *Side of Impurity* (§15 above). The meaning of *support two sides* would then be: Judgement is constitutive of both the Holy Chariot of the Divine Name, and of the destructive forms of the *Sitra Achra*.

Line 292: *They are the Ten Sephirot, the Ten Utterances*

According to the texts which continue *"and all the chariots are . . . Ten Sephirot, Ten Utterances"*, the word *"they"* above must refer to the Holy Names themselves. This would then be another reference to the *Upper and Lesser Sephirot* mentioned above line 196 (and notes there). According to MS. O, *"they"* would seem to refer only to the chariots.

For the phrase *the Ten Utterances*, see *the Ethics of the Fathers* 5.1.

Lines 301–302: *the World to Come*

*The World to Come* is often a symbol for the first letter *he*.

Line 323: *the Kindnesses of David*

The phrase derives from Isaiah 55:3; cf. Zohar vol.1 8a and 219a.

Line 324: *Tsvaot*

One of the Holy Names which may not be erased. See above, notes to l.191

Line 332: *the supports of the Torah*

Cf. SLDN 1.490 and Zohar vol.1 8a.

## NOTES TO TRANSLATION

**Key to Translation of Divine Attributes**

Deut.10.9

| | | |
|---|---|---|
| | great | גדול |
| | mighty | גבור |
| | awesome | נורא |

Ex.34.6–7

| | | |
|---|---|---|
| | merciful | רחום |
| | gracious | חנון |
| | slow to anger | ארך אפים |
| | abounding in kindness | רב חסד |
| | faithful | אמת |
| | extends kindness | נוצר חסד |
| | visits iniquity | פוקד עון |

Micah 7.18

| | | |
|---|---|---|
| | forgives iniquity | נושא עון |
| | remits transgression | עובר על פשע |

Isaiah 57.15

| | | |
|---|---|---|
| | high | רם |
| | dwells forever | שוכן עד |
| | holy | קדוש |
| Ex.15.3 | man of war | איש מלחמה |
| Is.66.6 | deals retribution | משלם גמול |
| Jer.3.12 | compassionate | חסיד |

111

## NOTES TO TRANSLATION

| Jer.50.34 | powerful | חזק |
|---|---|---|
| Psalms | | |
| 7.10 | tests the heart | ובוחן לבות |
| 10.5 | lofty | מרום |
| 25.8 | good | טוב |
| | upright | ישר |
| 50.6 | judge | שופט |
| 68.6 | magistrate | דיין |
| 89.9 | strong | חסין |
| 93.4 | majestic | אדיר |
| 103.3 | forgiving | סולח |
| Job 36.5 | mighty in strength | כביר כח |

# THE DOCTRINE OF THE DIVINE NAME

## Part Three

## THE SECRETS OF THE LETTERS OF THE DIVINE NAME

### Commentary

## COMMENTARY

Introduction – ll. 1–8

Our capacity to understand and to tell the *mighty acts* of creation is limited both above and below. Above it is limited by the pure unknowable simplicity of the Creator. The closer one approaches the Transcendent Creator, the more indistinct, obscure, and unknowable these *mighty acts* become. The four letters of the Divine Name are obscure compared to the more specific and well defined chariots which emerge below them. The *Impression of Existence* upon which these obscure letters were originally engraved is even more obscure.[1]

Below, understanding is limited by the infinite multiplicity of creation. Nevertheless the totality of these distinct chariots may be traced back, step by step, to their roots in the finite and knowable chariots of the Divine Name. In between the obscure roots of the Name above and the unknowable infinite multiplicity below, the Zohar paints as clear a picture of this process as possible – from the highest point where coherent images can first be discerned, to the lowest point where this clarity and coherence is lost in the increasing confusion and gloom of the emerging finite universe.

The picture which the Zohar paints is woven around a single central image: the four letters of the Divine Name – *YHVH*.[2] This picture of the Name is a *map* of the transition between unknowable simplicity above and unknowable multiplicity below. This map is divided into three distinct parts: upper, middle, and lower. This division is reflected textually in the literary structure of *the Secrets of the Letters:*

> a. The first two letters, *yod* and *he*, represent the upper extreme: the Name as it first emerges from the absolute simplicity of the Transcendent Creator – *Mercy and Judgement united together as one*. They are treated together in a single textual unit with its own introductory and concluding passages (ll. 8–80). The presentation of letter *yod* leads smoothly into the

---

[1] *Creator* – §13 / *obscure* – §20a / *Impression of Existence* – notes line 4
[2] *Dialectic of four letters* – §§11 & 12

presentation of letter *he* with no formal sign that a transition has been made.

b. The final letter *he* represents the lower extreme: the Name in its final transition from the unity of the Divine Name into the multiplicity of the finite universe. It is the *Gateway* through which the totality of God's creative and providential powers must pass. It is treated in a separate textual unit with its own introductory and concluding passages (ll. 80–158).

c. Letter *vav* stands in the middle of this process. It represents the Name as the full expression of the dialectic of Mercy and Judgement – *after* the concept of Love achieves full expression, but *before* it begins to break apart into the finite multiplicity of the created universe. The treatment of letter *vav* is far more detailed than that of the other letters, and longer than the treatment of all three combined. As the centerpiece of the presentation, letter *vav* is placed last. Otherwise the presentation follows the order of the letters as they appear in the Divine Name itself.

This map is sketched in three "dimensions:" *vertical, horizontal,* and *ethical:* [3]

a. The *vertical* dimension relates any stage in the process to the stage which immediately precedes it. Every stage represents a link in a chain: it is the *explicit expression* of that which precedes it, on the one hand, and *contains implicitly* that which will be explicitly expressed below it, on the other.

b. The *horizontal* dimension defines the nature of the relation between Judgement and Mercy at any stage in the process.

c. The *ethical* dimension describes the kind of providential force (*wrath, revenge, kindness, absolute forgiveness*) to which any given stage corresponds.

---

[3]*Vertical* – §§16–20 / *horizontal* – §§21–23 / *ethical* – §§1–7

LETTER YOD

The limited goal of this commentary is to help the reader follow the interlocking steps of the process as they occur, without losing track of the conceptual and ethical significance of each step along the way. Sometimes this requires expanding upon obscure and enigmatic statements, sometimes a brief summary of overlong or repetitive passages. Sometimes it requires reordering complex descriptions in a more simplified and schematic form. Some passages require little or no comment, while other times a series of passages must be taken together as a unit.

I have attempted to be as brief as possible without falling into the trap of explaining the obscure with the even more obscure. Concepts assumed by the commentary or mentioned in passing, which have been explained either in the interpretive essay or in the notes to the translation, are indicated in the footnotes – the interpretive essay by section number (§) and the notes by line number.

**Letter Yod**

The Ascent and Descent of Letter Yod – ll. 8–15

*Vertically*, letter *yod* both *ascends and descends*. It *descends* in that it contains the implicit Judgement from which all the lower worlds will emerge. It *ascends* in that it is the expression of something which lies hidden above it, to which *it corresponds*. Since behind this first *primordial point* lie only the Transcendent Creator and His Eternal Will, any attempt to trace the roots of letter *yod* upward will only lead to the dissolution of all thought, speech, and knowledge.[4]

---

[4]*Ascend and descend* – §20e /*dissolution of thought in the infinite* – §13. As obscure as this first letter *yod* may be, it is only the expression of some pre-existent root, a higher *upper yod*, hidden within the Transcendent Creator or His Will, to which this lower letter *yod* corresponds. This highest pre-existent form of the letters of the Divine Name transcends all understanding of the ordered conceptual kind presented in this exposition. Its treatment is reserved for the most esoteric literature of the Zohar, the *Sifra DiTsniuta* (vol. 2 177a – *upper yod* within *Atika* / *lower yod* in *Za'ir Anpin*) and the *Idrot* (vol. 3 127a–145a, 287b–296b).

## COMMENTARY

*Horizontally*, letter *yod* represents the initial notion of Mercy which includes Judgement, but in which Judgement has no independent concrete expression. Since within this initial notion of Mercy, Judgement and Mercy have not yet been distinguished from each other, neither can be defined or grasped. Judgement and Mercy as unified within Mercy can only be known *indirectly*, as the roots of these notions which eventually emerge below as distinct forces. For this reason, letter *yod* is represented symbolically as the *root* of letter *vav* below.[5]

This is the meaning of the notion that the *six sides* (the balance between Judgement and Mercy achieved in letter *vav* below)[6] are *hidden away* within the *chariot* of letter *yod*. These symbols are developed in the following sections.

### The Three Sides of the Chariot of Letter Yod – ll. 15–27

Letter *yod* is divided into three *knots* – the upper tip, the lower tip, and the body of the letter which stands in the middle. These correspond to the three *sides* of letter *vav* – right, left, and middle. However, in letter *yod* there is no distinction between Judgement and Mercy, and hence no meaning to the symbolic distinction of *left* and *right*.[7] So when these *sides* are distinguished from each other, they are called simply *"another side."*

The first *side* corresponds to the *right side* in letter *vav*, the *side* of Mercy which is opposed to Judgement. Since letter *yod*, unlike its transcendent root, is part of the *revealed Name*, it includes some minimal element of Judgement. For this reason, it also includes some minimal element of opposition *between* Judgement and Mercy. This inclusion sets up the following dynamic:

> This *first sparkling*, which barely exists at all, includes some minimal element of opposition between Judgement and Mercy. Judgement begins to form a separate identity. With the emer-

---

[5] *Judgement implicit within Mercy* – §11b / *distinction and definition* – §9 / *indirect knowledge of yod and he* – end of §13

[6] Cf. SLDN ll.158–164

[7] *Three knots* – notes line 19(2) / *left and right* – §21

gence of an aspect of Judgement as an independent factor, the differentiation of left, right, and middle begins to form within this *first sparkling*. It contains within itself *three sparks* – the roots of left, right, and middle.

Judgement as such does not yet exist here. The only manifestation of darkness is to be found in the fact that the light begins to *differentiate internally*. So the *other side*, which emerges from the *second knot* (despite the fact that it corresponds to the *dark* side of letter *vav*), is *indistinguishable* from the first side described above. It behaves in an identical fashion: it *ascends, descends*, and forms *three sparks* within a single *sparkling*, which are *supports* below it.[8]

The *third knot*, which corresponds to the *middle side* of letter *vav* below, should represent the *balance* between the opposition of Mercy to Judgement and the resolution of that opposition. But in letter *yod* no such balance exists. The only concrete manifestation of Judgement here is the mere fact of differentiation itself: the light differentiates into two *sides* which are indistinguishable. When the middle comes to resolve and reconcile these two sides it finds a differentiation which has distinguished nothing. Consequently, the *third knot* collapses back into a single undifferentiated *sparkling* which does not put forth *three other sparks*. Despite its instability, the *third knot* represents the middle: the resolution of the opposition between Mercy and Judgement. For this reason, it is ultimately the *third knot* which causes limitation and finitude *(the Sand)* to be linked to the infinite light of the Lamp.[9]

Summary – ll. 28–31

The chariot of letter *yod* is hidden because there are as yet no firm distinctions within it which can be grasped.[10] Nevertheless, when it is examined more closely, it is seen to include the roots of the dialectic of Mercy which emerges below. These roots are

---

[8] *Judgement as differentiation* – §9 / *supports* – §19

[9] *Balance of opposition and resolution* – end of §12 / *resolution of opposition between Mercy and Judgement* – §10 / *sand* – §14

[10] *Hidden* – §20b

represented by these *nine supports*: the three *sparklings*, and the six *sparks* which emerge from the first two *sparklings*. The first *sparkling* represents the chariot as a whole. When it *shines downward*, the other eight aspects included within it *shine downward* also. As a whole, they represent the inclusion of Judgement within Mercy as *internal articulation* and *differentiation*.

### The Names of the Three Sides – ll. 32–42

*Ethically*, this stage and its nine supports represent pure Mercy: *forgiveness* which punishes no one, not even those who deserve it. This is the meaning of the verse: *"Before you, I will have compassion upon those whom I will have compassion, and have mercy upon those whom I will have mercy"* – God will have mercy upon whomever He wishes, irrespective of the relative weight of their merits or sins.[11]

These nine supports can only be grasped as the *roots* of the three sides of letter *vav* below. They cannot be known *directly* even by Moses himself, whose level of prophecy included the totality of letter *vav*. Moses could not grasp these nine supports of letter *yod* – for they are inherently unknowable.

Nevertheless, as *ethical* categories of God's providence they are very real: *"I will have compassion upon those whom I will have compassion, and have mercy upon those whom I will have mercy."* If God in fact bestows mercy and compassion upon those who do not deserve it, it matters little if these infinite mercies transcend understanding. They can still be sought through prayer and experienced in life. With respect to knowledge *they may not be defined by names*, but with respect to prayer and lived experience, *they may*.

## The First Letter He

### The Emergence of Letter He – ll. 42–52

As these *nine supports* extend downward, the *implicit inclusion* of Judgement within letter *yod* moves toward *explicit expression*. In this process, it is not the creative power of letter *yod* which is expressed,

---

[11]*Pure forgiveness* – §2; cf. *Guide* 1:54 and Babylonian Talmud Berachot 7a

but rather the creative power of the Transcendent Creator. Letter *yod*, as the highest aspect of the Revealed Name, is the first revelation of this creative power. The term *"the Infinite"* seems to be the name for the upper unknown root of these nine supports within the Creator or His Will. Letter *yod* is itself only a stage in the revelation of the *Infinite*. In the extension of the *nine supports* of letter *yod*, the creative potential of the *Infinite* takes another step toward realization.[12]

Judgement was manifest in letter *yod* only as the internal articulation and differentiation of Mercy. These various distinctions proved to be unstable and collapsed together into the simple notion of implicit Judgement. The first step towards the realization of this implicit Judgement is its isolation as an *independent aspect*, which can be distinguished from Mercy, if not yet separated from it. The *single light* which emerges from the collapse of all the insubstantial *sparks* of letter *vav* represents this beginning.

This transition is symbolized as the transformation of the chariot of letter *yod* from a *Nut* which encloses letter *yod* into a *Palace* within which letter *yod* dwells. Mercy and Judgement are still not *opposed* to each other, but they are beginning to be *distinguished from* each other. The King may belong within his Palace just as the kernel belongs within the shell of the Nut. But the King and his Palace are not organically united to the same degree as the shell and the kernel within the image of the Nut.

## The Chariots, Ascent, and Descent of Letter He – ll. 52–68

Both the first upper letter *he* and the lower final letter *he* represent transitions from unity to multiplicity. The first letter *he* marks a transition (within the unity of the Name) from the simplicity of pure undifferentiated Mercy (letter *yod*) to the articulate dialectic of Mercy and Judgement (letter *vav*). The lower final letter *he* marks the transition from the dialectical unity of the Divine Name to the opposition and multiplicity of the finite universe.

---

[12]*Transition from implicit to explicit Judgement* – §11c / *power of Transcendent Creator* – §14 / *the Infinite* – notes line 33

In both cases, these transitions are symbolized by certain *numbers*. The number *four* represents the special opposition of North, South, East, and West. The number *five* (the numerical value of letter *he*) represents the center point which pulls these opposing elements together into a single unity.[13]

*Horizontally*, letter *he* represents the independent aspect of Judgement which emerges from the concept of Mercy. It is the unitary source from which all opposition derives. It is also the unity within which opposition is ultimately resolved – for without the integration of unity and opposition, even finite opposition could not exist.[14] Therefore, letter *he* includes *five supports* in which the opposition of left and right is resolved, while these five give rise to *five lights* in which the opposition of left and right begins to emerge.

*Vertically*, letter *he* can be traced upwards toward infinity.[15] Then the *five* of letter *he* becomes *fifty* – the *fifty wonders which are beyond comprehension*. When traced downward, these *fifty* resolve into *five supports* within the single light of letter *he*.

### The Chain of Chariots / Summary of Letter He – ll. 68–80

The *five lights* which emerge from the *five supports* of letter *he* mediate between the unity of letter *he* and the multiplicity of letters *vav* and final letter *he* (North, South, East, West) below.[16] These five lights begin to manifest the opposition of left and right. Therefore each light begins to define a specific identity in opposition to all the others. The five supports from which they emerge do not manifest this opposition. So each of the five supports includes all five distinct aspects (*lights*) which differentiate immediately below them. As a result these five lights and five supports add up to *twenty five* chariots for letter *he*, and not merely *ten* chariots.

---

[13]*Numbers* – §17 / *NSEW* – §17e

[14]*Existence as integration of identity and difference* – end of §9

[15]*Motion from infinity to finitude* – end of §17

[16]*Vav and he as NSEW* – §22

## The Final Letter He

### Introductory Verses – ll. 80–83

The final letter *he* of the Name represents the full expression of finitude and opposition as an independent principle within the unity of the Divine Name. Final letter *he* represents the unity *within* multiplicity that makes finite existence possible. But it also represents the root of multiplicity within unity that makes the reconciliation of finitude with the infinite possible. Therefore the Zohar emphasizes and reemphasizes that God is present within final letter *he* just as He is present within the *first ones*.[17]

### The Structure of He and its Chariot – ll. 84–93

Final letter *he* is structurally parallel to the first letter *he*. It represents a transition from unity (*five*) to multiplicity (*four*). Final letter *he* marks the transition from the unity of the Divine Name to the multiplicity of that which stands *outside* the unity of Divine Name. The four elements mentioned here belong to the lower world. They are only included in the unity of the upper world of the Divine Name *in so far as* they are unified within the final letter *he*. But in so far as they each maintain their own separate identities in the world of multiplicity, they belong to the lower non-Divine world. Therefore each corner of this chariot is a distinct being. Each has its own personal name: *Michael, Gabriel, Rafael, Uriel.*

### The Providential Forces of Letter He: Good and Evil – ll. 93–107

Final letter he represents two radically different possibilities:[18]

a. If the finite world freely returns God's love, then it is integrated (as a free and independent reality) into the higher unity of Divine Love. As the final positive integration of

---

[17]*Independence of Judgement* – §11f / *existence as integration of identity and difference* – end of §9 / *root of Judgement with Mercy* – §11

[18]*Two possibilities implicit in the notion of finitude* – §11f & g / *evil as residue* – §15 / *harsh Judgement* – §§4–5

Judgement and Mercy, this unity relegates the destructive negativity of Judgement to the netherworld of Gehinnom as the unfortunate but necessary residue of the creative process.

b. If the finite world, exercising its freedom, rejects God's love, then it separates itself from God, and divides the concrete manifestation of Judgement from its root within Mercy. This leaves the destructive negativity of Judgement unrestrained by God's Mercy and free to exact evil and cruel Judgement in the world.

If negativity is *not* integrated into Mercy by love, then this negativity sets up an opposition between the finite and the infinite, which separates between God and the world like a *hard and evil shell*. But if negativity is integrated into Mercy by love, then the same negativity becomes a vehicle for the full expression of that love, and *the evil shell passes away* – it no longer encloses the light of God's goodness.

### The Inseparability of Letters and Chariots – ll. 107–113

Every letter of the Divine Name represents an essential aspect of the dialectic of Mercy and Judgement.[19] From these root hypostases further aspects of God's creative and providential power necessarily differentiate downward. For this reason God is called *YHVH Tsvaot* – "the Lord of Hosts" – for all the miriad hosts of created beings which emerge from the Divine Name are in truth no more than an explication of the implicit meaning of the Name itself.

### The Inclusion of Lower Powers in the Final Letter He – ll. 113–124

The progressive differentiation of more and more concrete aspects of God's creative power eventually gives rise to the infinite multiplicity of the created world. In this way, all the elements of creation are ultimately included within the Divine Name. But the connection between these lower beings and the Divine Name is

---

[19] *Letters as hypostases of dialectic* – §12

mediated by long chains of intermediate steps and stages. They are all included, but not directly.

This notion of inclusion is not transitive. If the lower powers are included in final letter *he*, and final letter *he* is included in letter *vav* this does not mean that the lower powers are included in letter *vav*. Rather, each letter includes only that which immediately emerges from it.

An upper letter can be included in the lower powers only through the mediation of the various *palaces* which are interposed between them. If these palaces are linked and unified one to another, then the upper letters become *accessible* (indirectly) to those below. But the distinction between above and below cannot be overcome.

### The Upper Mysteries in the Final Letter He – ll. 124–142

The final letter *he* is the *Gateway* through which the totality of God's creative and providential powers pass, as they emerge from the unity of the Divine Name into the multiplicity of the finite universe. All the various forms which the dialectic of Mercy and Judgement assumes in the course of its development, are received by, and appear within, final letter *he*.

### Creation of Lower Worlds with Final Letter He – ll. 143–158

After final letter *he* receives all of these various forms from the worlds above it, it creates with them all of the lower worlds which exist below it. At this point the upper world of the Divine Name leaves off, and the finite World of Separation (the angels and the physical universe) begins.[20]

## Letter Vav

### Introduction to Letter Vav

The dialectic of Mercy and Judgement finds full expression only in letter *vav*. Letters *yod* and *he* are only the inarticulate roots of this dialectic. In final letter *he* the dialectic breaks down as the

---

[20]*Creation of lower worlds with final letter he* – notes to ll.152–153

various elements emerge into the finite world of separation as distinct and antithetical forms. The flow of the dialectic itself *which holds these elements together in an organic unity* is only clearly discernible in letter *vav*.

As we already mentioned above, the treatment of letter *vav* in *the Secrets of the Letters* is far more detailed and complex than the treatment of the other letters. The same three dimensions, the *vertical*, the *horizontal*, and the *ethical*, are mapped out here. But unlike the other three letters, this mapping proceeds in *three parallel lines* (left, right, and middle), each of which passes through *identical systematic stages*. In each of these three parallel lines, the same three dimensions are mapped out, each element in its proper place.

The Zohar certainly expects the reader to remember the corresponding elements from each of the three parallel lines, and to take note of both the similarities and the subtle differences between them. However, each of these parallel lines is quite long, and the distance between the corresponding elements can obscure both the similarities and the differences. For this reason, the commentary to letter *vav* will not follow the text in order. Rather it will examine the *vertical*, the *horizontal*, and the *ethical* dimensions separately, bringing together and comparing the corresponding passages from each of the three sides. Afterward, it will bring the different dimensions together into a synthetic picture of the entire dialectical process.

**The Vertical Dimension**

In letter *vav* the dialectic of Mercy and Judgement differentiates into three sides. The middle represents the concept of Mercy which overcomes opposition and so includes Judgement within itself. The right and the left represent Mercy and Judgement as opposites. This opposition develops immanently within the notion of Mercy as the necessary corollary of the concept of Judgement which was already seen to be included within Mercy.

From the singular *middle*, two opposites emerge: *right* and *left*. Since the opposition of right to left is an expression of Judgement, their emergence is depicted as linear motion away from the original source of Mercy above. So within letter *vav*, vertical motion always takes the same form: *a single entity differentiates into two other entities – one to its right and one to its left below it.*

The Zohar's description of letter *vav* traces this vertical process through *four distinct stages* on each of the three sides. These stages are systematically arranged and are designated by easily recognizable formula. With regard to these stages and formula, the three sides are virtually identical to each other. The differences between the sides relate either to the *ethical* or to the *horizontal* dimensions, and so will be treated below in their proper places.[21]

Stage One – right: ll. 164–171 / left: ll. 207–211 / middle: ll. 256–262

Right      The first phase on the right side – the mystery of the Primordial Light.

Left      The first phase on the left side – the mystery of the Darkness which extends in darkness downward, until glowing Hell is created from that darkness of harsh, red–black fire.

Middle      The first phase on the middle side is in the Eastern Gate, for the Eastern Gate stands in the middle. It takes two sides to join them together ... on both this side and the other.

Each of the three sides begins with a single simple entity. The right begins with *pure light* with no admixture of darkness – i.e. Mercy unsullied by any admixture of Judgement. The left begins with the pure *red–black darkness* of the fires of Hell – i.e. pure unmitigated harsh Judgement. The middle begins with a third simple, undifferentiated entity – the simple notion of *infinite Mercy* which resolves the opposition of Judgement and Mercy, including both together in its simple unity.

---

[21]*Opposition within Mercy* – §11b & c / *linear motion* – introduction to §16

COMMENTARY

Stage Two – right: ll. 171–184 / left: ll. 215–228 / middle: ll. 262–273

| | |
|---|---|
| Right | a spirit arises which blows with twelve spirits of incense |
| Left | another spirit . . . shines out of the Lamp . . . [which] does not arise with incense or with fragrance |
| Middle | the spirit arises which blows with twelve fragrances of incense |

These three sides each possess chariots from which the various entities implicitly contained within them will emerge. Both the right (which is opposed to Judgement) and the middle (which includes Judgement) have sweet smelling scents, for they are both notions of Mercy and goodness. The right is Mercy as a finite concept opposed to Judgement. The middle is Mercy as subsuming Judgement. Only the left, whose root is unmitigated destructive negativity, has no sweet scent.[22]

| | |
|---|---|
| Right | This [spirit] differentiates and becomes three . . . These three colors are one chariot for the right side in the mystery of letter *vav*. |
| Left | this spirit which differentiates into three colors . . . These three colors are one chariot for the left side in the mystery of letter *vav*. |
| Middle | When this spirit differentiates, it differentiates into three glowing colors . . . These three colors are one chariot in the mystery of letter *vav* |

In accordance with the principle explained above, each of these chariots differentiates into two others, arriving at the number *three*.

---

[22]*Chariot* – §19 / *Mercy as opposed to Judgement and as resolving this opposition* – §10 / *Judgement as destructive negativity* – §§4, 5, & 15

## LETTER VAV – VERTICAL DIMENSION

Stage Three – right: ll. 192–195 / left: ll. 232–236 / middle: ll. 285–295

Right  each one of these three colors differentiates into two others, to each side, until they arrive at the sum of *three times three*, which is *nine*, while the Right . . . completes [the number] *ten*.

Left  each one of these three colors differentiates into two others, to each side, until they arrive at the sum of *three times three*, which is *nine* . . . while the Left . . . completes [the number] *ten*.

Middle  each one of the three colors differentiates into two others, to each side, until they become the sum of *three times three* to each side, which is *nine*, while the Holy Name which rules over them completes [the number] *ten*.

Each of the three colors which emerge from the original chariot divides into two others, arriving at the number *nine*. If one adds to these nine chariots the original simple notions mentioned in the first phase of each side, one arrives at the number *ten* – *Ten Sephirot*.[23]

Stage Four – right: ll. 204–207 / left: ll. 242–249 / middle: ll. 307–310

Right  From these [colors], lights differentiate downward.

Left  From here on, countless *mighty acts* differentiate downward

Middle  From these [colors], lights differentiate downward

This process continues downward *ad infinitum*, producing the infinite multiplicity of the created universe.

---

[23] *Ten sephirot* – notes line 196

COMMENTARY

**The Ethical Dimension**

Each of these colors corresponds to a *Name* or an *attribute* of God. Each of these *attributes* has a specific ethical *(providential)* content which is appropriate to its place on either the left side of Judgement, the right side of Kindness *(Mercy as opposed to Judgement)*, or in the middle *(Mercy as subsuming Judgement)*. After describing the first two stages as an abstract process, the Zohar returns to give each of the entities which emerges in this process its proper concrete name.[24]

Names of First Two Stages – right: ll. 184–192 / left: ll. 228–232 / middle: ll. 273–285

| | |
|---|---|
| Right | This side, which is Right, is called *El*. Its chariot is called, in its totality, *Great*. When this chariot, which is these three colors, differentiates, they are the names which are called: *Great, Strong, Holy*. |
| Left | One is called *Majestic*, one is called *Powerful*, and, in its totality, it is called *Mighty*, because this side is called Left – it is *Elohim*. |
| Middle | This name ... is *YHVH*. Its chariot is called *Awesome* in its totality ... this chariot ... differentiates into three other colors ... *Awesome, Faithful, Extends Kindness* |

The *first phase* of each of the three sides corresponds to one of the Ten Holy Names of God which may not be erased.[25] They are *El* to the right, *Elohim* to the left, and *YHVH* in the middle:

**ELOHIM**            **YHVH**            **EL**

---

[24] *Names, attributes, words* – §16
[25] *Ten holy names* – notes line 191

## LETTER VAV – ETHICAL DIMENSION

Each of these Holy Names possesses a chariot. These three chariots are called *in their totality*: *Great* to the right, *Mighty* to the left,[26] and *Awesome* in the middle:

| **Mighty** | **YHVH** | **EL** |
|---|---|---|
| **ELOHIM** | **Awesome** | **Great** |

Each of these *general attributes* differentiates into two more specific attributes:

| Majestic | **YHVH** | **EL** |
|---|---|---|
| Powerful | **Awesome** | **Great** |
| **Mighty** | Faithful | Strong(Kind) |
| **ELOHIM** | Extends Kindness | Holy |

After describing at length the abstract process in which these nine attributes differentiate into twenty-seven attributes, the Zohar returns again to give each its name.

Names of Stage Three – right: ll. 196–204 / left: ll. 236–242 / middle: ll.295–307

Right     The two which emerge from the color in which Water predominates: one is called *merciful* and the other is called *gracious* . . . The two which emerge from the color in which Fire predominates: one is called *slow to anger* and the other is called *abounding in kindness* . . . The two which emerge from the color in which Air predominates: one is called *kind* and the other is called *forgiving*.

Left     The two which emerge from . . . the color of *darkness*: one is called *judge* and the other is called *magistrate* . . . The two which emerge from . . . the Red Fire: one is called *mighty in strength* and the other is called *man of war*. The two which emerge from . . . the Black Fire:

---

[26]For the reversed hierarchy of the attributes on the left side see notes 1.195.

COMMENTARY

one is called *visits iniquity* and the other is called *deals retribution*.

Middle     The two which emerge from one point: one is called *forgives iniquity* and the other is called *remits transgression* ... The two which emerge from the color in which Fire predominates: one is called *lofty* and the other is called *high* ... The two which emerge from the third color, in which Air predominates: one is called *dwells forever* and the other is called *holy*.

Out of the first three stages of this process, the following list of thirty Names and attributes has emerged:

| ELOHIM | YHVH | EL |
|---|---|---|
| Majestic | **Awesome** | Great |
| judge | forgives iniquity | merciful |
| magistrate | remits transgression | gracious |
| Powerful | Faithful | Strong(Kind) |
| mighty in strength | lofty | slow to anger |
| man of war | high | abounding in kindness |
| **Mighty** | Extends Kindness | Holy |
| visits iniquity | dwells forever | compassionate |
| deals retribution | holy | forgiving |

The Zohar gives no names to the entities which emerge in stage four, because they are infinite. But it is clear that, in principle, they branch out to include all the attributes applied to God, and from there to encompass all the words included in the Bible.[27]

### The Horizontal Dimension

In letter *vav*, Judgement first achieves explicit concrete manifestation. With this first manifestation of Judgement, the radical and

---

[27] Cf. the passage from *Shaare Orah* quoted in §16.

absolute opposition of pure Judgement and pure Mercy also appears. The *horizontal dimension* of letter *vav* is the gradual, step by step *reintegration* of Judgement into Mercy *(the sweetening of Judgement)* by the harmonizing and reconciling force of the middle.[28] The third and fourth stages of this process are merely mechanical repetitions of the first two stages and add nothing to the understanding of the horizontal dimension. Therefore this section of the commentary will limit itself to an examination of the first two stages on each of the three sides.

The process begins with the *unmediated extremes* of left and right and with the *abstract middle* which has not yet succeeded in mitigating their absolute opposition.

Stage One – right: ll. 164–171 / left: ll. 207–211 / middle: ll. 256–262

Right
: *The first phase on the right side – the mystery of the Primordial Light.*

Left
: *The first phase on the left side – the mystery of the Darkness which extends in darkness downward, until glowing Hell is created from that darkness of harsh, red-black fire. Here harsh flashes glow, which well up and are drawn downward.*

Middle
: *The first phase on the middle side is in the Eastern Gate, for the Eastern Gate stands in the middle. It takes two sides to join them together with beams and doors, on both this side and the other. This Gate includes all those which we have mentioned ... This is vav, the totality of them all. It exists in the mystery of all six upper sides.*

The right side is the unbroken pure light of the beginning. With the extension of this light, Judgement begins to emerge. From the first harsh flashes which begin to glow here, an entire river of harsh red-black fire flows forth until it reaches the depths of Gehinnom.

---

[28]*Sweetening of Judgement* – §15

COMMENTARY

At this stage, the middle is no more than the sum of these two extremes, the unity out of which they differentiate in opposition to each other. But as such, it is also the unity into which they will eventually be (partially) reintegrated.[29]

### The Second Stage on the Right Side – ll. 171–184

> *a spirit arises which blows with twelve spirits of incense, raising a fragrance, yet not raising it. [This chariot] includes three colors ... One glows with Fire, one glows with Water, and one glows with Air. [But] ... they are not Fire, or Water, or Air. Rather ... each one shines, and glows, and strengthens the place which is above it ... the Fire which is included in the right side ... the Water which is included in the right side ... the Air which is included in the right side ...*

The light of the right side begins to differentiate into three colors. This is only possible by the introduction of an element of darkness. As in letter *yod* above, this inclusion of darkness is limited to *internal differentiation* and *articulation*. The three elements which develop here are not fire, water, and air,[30] but rather different aspects *which strengthen the place above it* – i.e. three shades of light. The Mercy of the right side continues to exclude Judgement from itself. Nevertheless, the fact that three different stable shades of light have been distinguished on the right side shows that the exclusion of Judgement from Mercy has been mitigated somewhat, and that their absolute opposition to each other is beginning to be mediated.[31]

---

[29] *River of fire* – Daniel 8.9–10 / *emergence of harsh Judgement* – §15 / *extension* – §17c
[30] Notes to ll.190, 220–222
[31] *Judgement as differentiation* – §9 / *fire, air, water* – §23

## LETTER VAV – HORIZONTAL DIMENSION

### Transition to Stage Two on the Left Side – ll. 211–215

> *When the Lamp arises out of the measuring of the Measuring Line, it shines to the right side. From that shining, it shines to this side, toward the Darkness – and lights approach this Fire. They draw the Fire closer to the Right, and [the Darkness] is infused with its light.*

Unlike the right side (which spontaneously differentiates into three different shades of light), the left side must wait for an outside stimulus before anything positive can occur within the pure negativity of wrathful Judgement. The light of the right (which had extended) already contained a minimal element of Judgement – and with it the roots of its own differentiation. But the left side of pure Judgement is nothing but absolute opposition to Mercy. Nothing within this pure negativity would bring it to approach the light of Mercy. Only the external influence of the light of Mercy would cause it to begin to approach the right side. As it begins to approach the right, an element of light is introduced into this darkness, and the darkness becomes visible for the first time.

### Stage Two on the Left Side – ll. 215–228

> *Then another spirit . . . extends, in the mystery of three colors, toward that side which is called North. But this spirit does not arise with incense or with fragrance, because it is the Left which rests upon this spirit which differentiates into three colors.*

The Mercy of the middle partially mitigates the absolute opposition between Judgement and Mercy. This allows a partial infusion of the light of the right side into the left. But just as the limited introduction of darkness into the right side did not yield Judgement, but rather only the internal differentiation of Mercy, so also on the left: the result is only the internal differentiation of Judgement. These three aspects of Judgement remain destructive in their essence, and so do not have a sweet fragrance of incense.

COMMENTARY

> *These colors shine in the three sides of Fire, which is the left side: Fire the color of darkness, Fire the color of red, Fire the color of black ... Fire the color of darkness which is on the left side ... Fire the color of red which is on the left side ... Fire the color of black which is on the left side*

Just as there was no presence of fire on the right side, so also there is no presence of water on the left side – only *three kinds of fire*. And just as it was virtually impossible to tell the different aspects of light within letter *yod* apart, so also, within letter *vav*, it is not clear what distinguishes these different shades of light from each other, on the right, or these different shades of darkness from each other, on the left.[32]

Following the analogy of a visual image, the first phase on the left is like absolute darkness in which nothing can be seen, whereas the second stage is like a deep gloom in which vague shapes appear, but no distinct form can be clearly identified. Similarly, the first phase on the right is like a brilliant and unbroken light in which nothing can be seen, while the second stage is like an intense light which nevertheless contains some contrast: again vague shapes can be discerned, but no distinct forms can be made out.[33]

Stage Two on the Middle Side – ll. 262-273

> *This [side] stands on a chariot which is three, including both Right and Left.*

The chariot of the middle contains three elements, just like the right and the left. But unlike the right and the left, the chariot of the middle includes both fire and water. Since it contains both of them, the contrast between them allows them to appear clearly for the first time. Fire as it appears in the chariot of the left is always qualified by the words *"which is on the left side."* Water on the right is qualified as the water *"which is included on the right side."* Without

---

[32]Notes to ll.190, 220–222

[33]*Visual image* – §9

the actual inclusion of fire on the right, even water cannot appear clearly. Similarly without the actual presence of water on the left, even fire cannot appear clearly. Only in the middle, which mediates the opposition of left and right, bringing them into proximity to each other, are *fire* and *water* mentioned without any qualifying phrases:

> *When this spirit differentiates, it differentiates into three glowing colors: Fire, Water, and Air, just like on the right side. But when it differentiates, each one glows in its own place, and the brilliance, which extends from this spirit, strengthens each of these three sides. The first color glows with Fire and it strengthens it. The second color glows with Water and it increases it. The third color glows with Air and it infuses it with a light, like purple – glowing with these two sides.*

The middle shines brightly with sweet smelling colors, just like the right. But on the right the clear differentiation of three distinct elements was suppressed, since Judgement (which is the source of finite differentiation) was excluded from the right side. The middle, which includes Judgement, differentiates into three distinct elements each of which clearly manifests its own essence. Nevertheless, as Mercy, the middle brings them together into a harmonious balance.

The left side is the fire of Judgement as integrated into Mercy – *faithful, lofty,* and *high.* The right side represents the waters of Mercy – *forgiving iniquity* and *remitting transgression.* The middle glows with both of these two sides – the infinite Mercy of the beginning. The middle remains constant throughout the entire process. The left and the right emerge from the middle. Left and right are gradually reintegrated by the harmonizing power of the middle. But the middle itself remains unchanged throughout it all.

### The Name of the First Stage on the Middle Side – ll. 273-285

> *Even though this [side] is called by letter vav, it subsumes all the names, upper and lower – all four letters of the Holy*

## COMMENTARY

*Name are unified in it, because it subsumes all sides, above and below. This is the mystery of YHV. This name belongs here, and it is YHVH. It takes two letters above and one below, and it stands in the middle, between above and below, and [between] the two sides as we have said.*

This middle is the dialectical balance of identity and difference, of finitude and infinity. It is the root out of which the whole emerges, and, even as the various elements of this dialectic develop around it, it remains unchanged – the center which continues to unify the whole as one.

### Summary

*Vertically,* once one has grasped the principle involved, the entire treatment of letter *vav* is seen to be no more than the trivial repetition of the same pattern of *differentiation downward.*

*Ethically,* relatively little occurs on the right as it is gradually brought closer to the middle, since both the right and the middle represent Mercy.[34] On the left, however, a radical transformation takes place. The initial phase on the left was pure radical, destructive wrath – *evil.* The second stage was still wrath, but turned to its proper use in punishing the wicked – *the Judge of orphans and widows.* Finally in the middle, the strength and violence of fire has been *sublimated* – transformed into strength of purpose and *faithfulness* within Mercy itself.

This integration and neutralization of the destructive violence of the left is only made possible by a parallel (if less noticeable) transformation of the right. This *parallel horizontal motion* is the key to understanding the ethical transformation which occurs in letter *vav.* It will provide the focus for this synthetic summary.

Within letter *vav,* the *light* and *darkness* of the extremes of right and left are gradually transformed into the *water* and *fire* of the middle. The images of water, fire, and air represent the *interpenetration* and *integration* of Mercy and Judgement. Water "contains"

---

[34]Cf. *Shekel HaKodesh* pp. 53–54

fire, and fire "contains" water. That which appears as water is only an admixture of the two in which the element of water *predominates*. That which appears as fire is only an admixture of the two in which the element of fire *predominates*.[35]

In the lower world this unity of the elements is reflected *quantitatively* as the differing proportions of the distinct elements within any given body. In the upper world the unity of the elements is expressed *qualitatively* as the integration of identity and difference which gives rise to coherent qualitative distinctions.

It is only through fire that water is known as and *is* water. It is only through water that fire is known as and *is* fire. Since they need each other in order to exist, they are unified. But since they only exist as distinct elements through their opposition to each other, they are separate. This is the true notion of the interpenetration of the elements as it exists in the upper world. The quantitative interpenetration of the elements in the lower world is only an *approximation* of this notion under the conditions of extreme Judgement which prevail in the lower physical world of non-contradiction.[36]

The transformation of Mercy and Judgement as absolute opposites (light and darkness) into Mercy and Judgement as mutually integrated and interpenetrating elements (fire and water) occurs in three steps. The middle itself is not directly affected by this transformation. All explicit motion is *from the extremes* of left and right *toward the middle:*

*The first step* (Stage One on the left and the right) represents the extreme opposition of the pure unrestrained wrath of Hell to the pure unsullied forgiveness of the World to Come. In neither the extreme right nor the extreme left can any form be discerned. They represent absolute unbroken light and darkness respectively.

---

[35]*Interpenetration and predominance* – §23

[36]*Water and fire, identity and opposition* – §9 (Midrash Temurah cited) / *opposition as ruling lower world, resolution upper world* – §§8 & 10 and Zohar vol. 2 24b

COMMENTARY

*The second step* (Stage Two on the left and the right) represents the mitigation of the opposition between Mercy and Wrath. Both the left and the right move slightly toward the center. A minimal element of light is introduced into the left, and a minimal element of darkness is introduced into the right. Internal differentiation results from the introduction of contrast between light and darkness. Nevertheless, the elements fire, air, and water do not appear.

*The third step* (Stage Two in the middle): As the left and right approach the middle, they appear as fire and water – *distinct, fully formed elements which interpenetrate and are integrated within the unity of the middle.*

These three steps have been schematized (in the diagram on the following page) in the following manner:

The first step of *absolute opposition* is at the top of the diagram, with the extremes of Judgement and Mercy placed at the extremes of left and right. The notion that only the roots of absolute Judgement exist above, while its full manifestation is found only below, is represented by the dotted lines leading downward on the left side. These two extremes are correlated with the category of *formlessness* at the bottom of the diagram.

In the second step of *relative opposition* the three differentiated forms of light and darkness are placed below the extremes of left and right and are moved inwards toward the center. The elements here are *semi-formed* as is indicated at the bottom of the diagram.

In the third step of *integration of opposition and unity* the elements fire and water appear *fully formed* and are united together within the middle circle.

This diagram represents the dialectic of Mercy and Judgement as depicted in the concrete terms of the symbols and dimensions which the Zohar and his contemporaries employed.

## LETTER VAV – SUMMARY

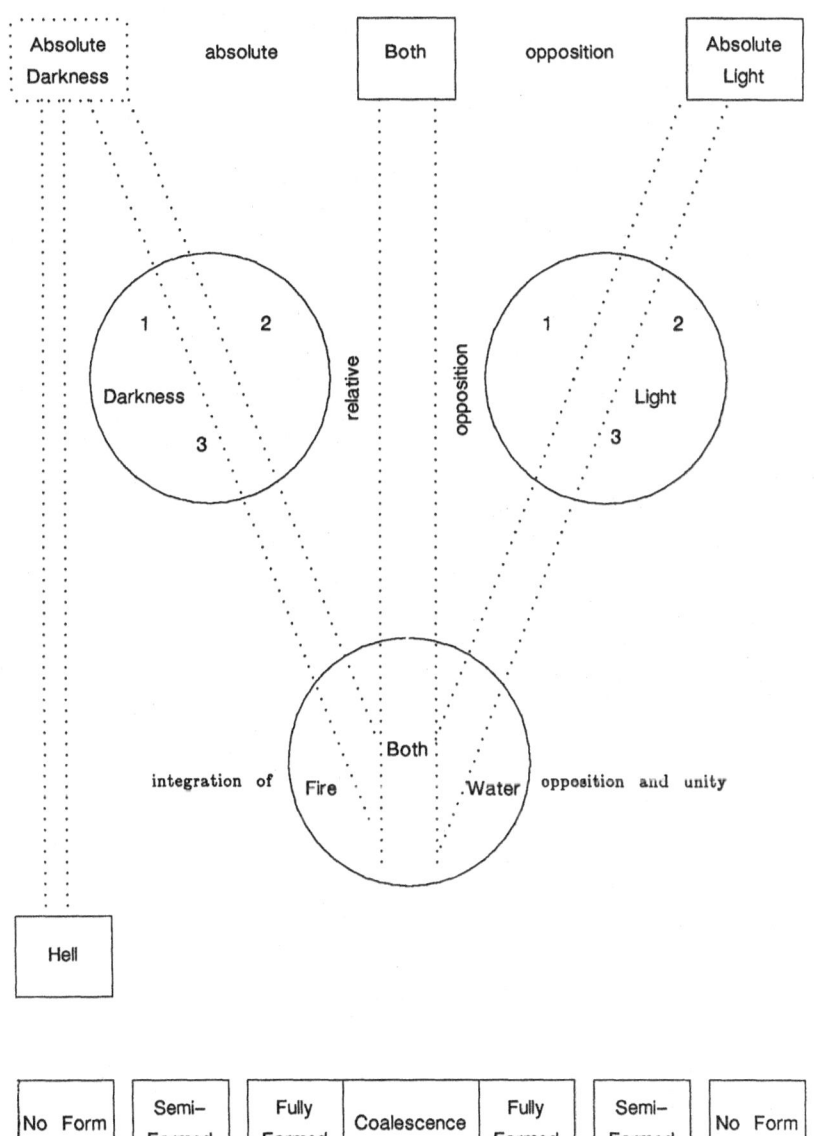

141

## COMMENTARY

As the extremes of fire and water approach the middle, *the concrete manifestation of their attributes grows stronger, while the opposition between them weakens*. If Judgement and Kindness were originally two separate and antithetical forces this could never occur. One cannot understand this process by starting from the opposing extremes and then attempting to bring them together artificially. Ultimately this approach leads to metaphysical dualism. If the ethical ramifications of this approach are thought through (and accepted) it could also lead to moral dualism and Gnostic antinomianism.[37]

The Zohar takes a different approach. He traces these opposing principles back to their source in a stage which *precedes* the opposition itself. He takes the middle as his starting point: Infinite Mercy which includes both principles as unified within itself. Only at a later stage does the opposition of the extremes develop out of this unity. By following this process through its various stages he shows the essential relativity of the opposition between Mercy and Judgement. In this way, he can maintain, both intellectually and spiritually, the traditional Jewish ideals of integration and harmony between Justice and Mercy, on the one hand, and between *This World* and the *World to Come* on the other.[38]

---

[37] *Dualism* – §1

[38] *Relativity* – §10 / *justice and life in this world as religious values* – §3 / *tensions and contradictions in rabbinic thought* – §6

## THE THREE LOWER SIDES

Appendix: The Three Lower Sides – ll. 310-334

The three lower sides are not developed in *the Secrets of the Letters*, and it is not clear where they fit in the overall conceptual scheme. The little treatment they receive is largely symbolic, and by tracing the parallel symbols both in the Zohar and in contemporary kabbalistic writings, it is not difficult to fill in this sketchy symbolic picture. But the following brief passage constitutes the only abstract statement made concerning their place in the dialectic of Mercy and Judgement:

> *In a like manner, there are three sides which emerge from these upper sides which we have mentioned, which are Right, Left, and Middle. These extend further out than these – two of them extend ... These lower [sides] which emerge from these upper sides, which we have mentioned, are precisely comparable to them – one is called Right, one is called Left, and one which stands in the middle within that Middle which we have mentioned.*

If they are precisely comparable, what do they add? If they are different, in what way are they different? The only difference explicitly mentioned is that the left and the right of these three lower sides extend outward, while the middle remains within the middle of the upper three sides.

*Symbolically*, this refers to the notion that the *legs*, which correspond to the *arms* above, extend outward beyond the body, whereas the point in the lower half of the body where the legs meet is continuous with the body itself.[39]

*Conceptually*, I would posit the following conjecture: The left and the right sides of the first three upper sides were not completely formed – they were stages which *preceded* the clear articulation of fire, water, and air. These three distinct elements appear first within the middle side above. Since the middle of the first three upper sides contains implicitly all three sides as fully formed, it is reasonable to

---

[39] *Arms and body* – §21 / *legs* – cf. SLDN ll.487-490

assume that the two fully formed sides of left and right should emerge from this middle and stand independently in their own right.

If this conjecture is correct, it would mean that the right side of the lower three sides represents *Kindness* as fully articulated and integrated with Judgement, yet standing independently in its own right. The left side of the lower three sides would represent *Judgement* as fully articulated and integrated with Kindness, yet standing independently in its own right. The *Middle* out of which these two emerge would be identical to the middle side of the first three upper sides, except that instead of being viewed *horizontally* as mediating between the extremes of harsh Judgement and pure Mercy, it would be viewed *vertically* as turning downward and expressing that which is contained implicitly within it.

# THE DOCTRINE OF THE DIVINE NAME

## Part Four:

## THE SECRETS OF THE LETTERS OF THE DIVINE NAME

### Aramaic Text

## THE ARAMAIC TEXT OF SLDN

### The Manuscripts of SLDN[1]

Among those relatively early (15th century) manuscripts which Tishbi[2] characterized as especially important, only one was found to contain the text of SLDN: MS.Bodl.Or.574 fol. 43r–48r, in the possession of the Bodleian Library of Oxford University.[3] The Curators of the Bodleian Library have kindly granted me permission to publish this text. It has been chosen to serve as the basis of the critical text presented below. In the translation, this manuscript is referred to as MS. O.

A second text of SLDN is found in manuscript Mic. 1761 fol.24a–27b in the possession of the Jewish Theological Seminary of America. Permission to use this manuscript in the preparation of the critical text has been granted by courtesy of the Library of the Jewish Theological Seminary of America. In the translation, this manuscript is referred to as MS. S., and in the critical text by the letter ס.

### The First Edition of SLDN

The Zohar was first printed virtually simultaneously in both Cremona and Mantua between the years 1558 to 1560.[4] Despite the numerous manuscripts which the printers in Mantua claimed to have in their possession, none of them seemed to contain a text of SLDN. The printers in Cremona, however, did manage to include the text of SLDN in their edition, from pages 12a–14b (columns 45–55).

---

[1]The present state of the Aramaic text of the Zohar is unfortunately still quite unsatisfactory. Other than the present edition of SLDN, not a single page of the Zohar has been edited critically. There is not even a catalogue of the contents of extant manuscripts, such that finding a particular text like SLDN in the confused and disordered maze of any given Zohar manuscript is largely a matter of chance.

[2]*Mishnat HaZohar* vol. 1 p. 110.

[3]Tishbi (ibid) refers to this manuscript by the number Oxford 1564. Kadari (*Grammar*, pp.177–180) also used this manuscript in his brief comparison of various Zohar texts.

[4]See Meir Benayahu, *Hebrew Printing at Cremona, Its History and Bibliography* (Jerusalem 1971) pp. 119–138.

## THE SECRETS OF THE LETTERS

This text represents a third independent text of SLDN, and so has been included in the critical apparatus. In the translation it is referred as ZC, and in the critical apparatus by the letter ק.

MS. O has been reproduced as accurately as possible, excluding those very few obvious scribal errors which are corrected in the body of the manuscript itself. The alternative readings from MS. S. likewise exclude such corrected errors. Similarly, alternatives which have only phonological significance have been excluded. Otherwise all alternative readings, no matter how trivial or how mistaken they may appear, have been recorded in the critical apparatus.

### First Edition of Zohar Hadash

Zohar Hadash was first published in Salonika in 1597. Zohar Hadash is a collection of those Zohar texts which the printers in Cremona and Mantua did not include in their editions of the Zohar. Apparently by this early date preference had already been given to the Mantua edition of the Zohar, for the Zohar Hadash also contains certain texts, like SLDN, which are contained in Cremona, but lacking in Mantua. The text of SLDN in ZHS seems to have been published from the Cremona edition, supplemented by a manuscript similar to MS. S. This conclusion seems warranted by the following evidence:

A. Strange readings and obvious errors found only in ZC which are reproduced exactly in ZHS:

line 28 עלמא instead of על מה;

line 51 סמיכין instead of סמכין;

line 73 על instead of כל;

line 150 בלבא instead of בכלא (בכלא cited in ZHS as alternative);

line 194 על דעאלו instead of עד דעאלו;

lines 226–227 the third group of the left side is omitted by accident (in ZHS it is cited as an alternative reading);

B. Both manuscripts of SLDN break off in the middle of a sentence. ZC smooths off the ending by omitting the entire sentence fragment. ZHS ends as in ZC, citing the reading of the manuscripts as an alternative.

## ARAMAIC TEXT

C. The passage which follows SLDN in ZC is printed in ZHS following SLDN. The passage which follows SLDN in MS. S. is mentioned parenthetically, and the reader is referred to the place in the Mantua edition where it is to be found.

D. None of the characteristic readings of MS. O. are to be found in ZHS. For example:

line 1 the full title is to be found only in MS. O.;

line 4 סתימן instead of רשימן;

line 115 אית instead of לית;

line 118 לכל instead of לבר;

line 190 חסיד instead of חסין;

This evidence indicates that ZHS is based on ZC. Where it deviates from ZC, it tends to conform to the readings found in MS. S. As a result it cannot be considered an independent textual witness.

Moreover, as Tishbi has already pointed out,[5] ZHS is hopelessly corrupt and cannot be relied upon to transmit any readings faithfully. One striking example of this will suffice:

Lines 146 to 150 are copied twice in ZHS by mistake. The first time the word *izdamna* is spelled with a final *aleph* which could be either feminine singular or plural. The second time it is spelled with a final *tav* which could only be singular. This type of morphological difference would normally have been recorded in the critical apparatus. But ZHS clearly cannot be trusted to record such distinctions accurately.

For these two reasons ZHS has been held to be of little or no critical value and has not been considered in the preparation of either the critical edition or the translation.

### Later Editions of Zohar Hadash[6]

Zohar Hadash was reprinted in 1603 in Cracow. This edition is virtually identical to the Salonika edition, and its critical worth is no different.

---

[5]*Mishnat HaZohar* vol. 1 p. 110.

[6]See Scholem, *Bibliographia Kabbalistica* (Leipzig 1927) p. 175 ff.

In 1658 Zohar Hadash was reprinted again in Venice from the earlier editions. But this time it was substantially corrected by the Kabbalist Rabbi Moses Zakuto. The 1702 Amsterdam edition is virtually identical to the Venice edition. These two editions contain many valuable readings, and since virtually all subsequent editions of SLDN have been based on them, these readings have been taken into account while preparing the translation. These readings are referred to as ZHV.

Finally the 1911 Munkatch edition is worthy of special note. Tishbi already has pointed out[7] that this late edition contains corrections from manuscript evidence. This assertion is born out by the alternative readings of this edition to lines 121, 252, and 329 of our text, which seem to preserve authentic additions of entire sentences which apparently have fallen out of all other extant texts. The readings of this edition, like those of the Venice edition, have also been used while preparing the translation. These readings are referred to as ZHM.

### The Ketem Paz

Finally, the textual emendations of Rabbi Shimon Lavi to SLDN should be mentioned. In the very beginning of his commentary to SLDN (Ketem Paz reprint Jerusalem 1981 vol. 1 pp. 261b–276b) Rabbi Shimon Lavi states that the text of SLDN has become terribly corrupt. He therefore transcribes the entire text of lines 1–42 before beginning his deep and exhaustive commentary. Tishbi has pointed out the critical value of the readings of the Ketem Paz.[8] They also have been consulted while preparing the translation. They are referred to as Ketem Paz. Needless to say, the commentary of Rabbi Shimon Lavi, as well as those of Rabbi Moses Zakuto and Rabbi Shalom Buzaglo to SLDN were of inestimable value in preparing this work.

Those readings from ZHV, ZHM, and the Ketem Paz used in the translation are given below in the original Aramaic.

---

[7]*Mishnat HaZohar* vol. 1 p. 110.

[8]*Mishnat HaZohar* vol. 1 p. 115.

## ARAMAIC TEXT

## Additional Alternative Readings Used in Translation

alternative reading / MS. O :line

11: תחותיה / *Ketem Paz* תחות

13: חדא תחותיה ההוא / *Ketem Paz* ZHM  חדא תחותיה . ההוא

15: סטרא / ZHV ZHM סתרא

19: וההוא נציצו / ZHM והוא חד נציצו / *Ketem Paz* נפקא חד נציצו

35: סלקין בשמא / ZHV ZHM *Ketem Paz* [ולא סלקין]

35: ורזא / ZHM [וקראתי בשם ח']

38: דיליה בההוא נציצו קדמאה כתי' / *Ketem Paz* דיליה דההוא נציצו קדמאה . ועל דא כתיב

40: וכל דא / ZHV ZHM *Ketem Paz* ועל דא

46: ואתחפייא / ZHV ZHM ואתחפיין

94: איהי למבכי / ZHV ZHM איהי עידן למבכי

96: בהאי קליפה / ZHV ZHM בהאי נקודה קליפא

105: קדמאה לה / ZHV ZHM קדמה לה

121: בגויה / ZHM [וכל שמא ושמא מן שמהן קדישין אתכליל רתיכא קדישא בגויה]

135: אזנין / ZHM אינון

146: דאתאחידת / ZHV ZHM דאית חדא

150: בהו / ZHV ZHM בה

150: ואיהי עמהון / ZHM [אלין דלסטר אתאחידת בה ואיהי עמהון . אלין דלסטר צפון אתאחידת עמהון ואיהי עמהון]

172: רוחין דבוסמין / ZHV רוחין

173: ריחא / ZHM רוחין ZHV ריחין

184: ו' / ZHV ZHM ח'

## THE SECRETS OF THE LETTERS

195: דרכיבי / ZHV ZHM רכיב

199: במיא / ZHV ZHM ביח מיא

212: כד / ZHV ZHM בר

212: נהיר לסטר / ZHV ZHM דנהיר מסטר

216: דנהיר / ZHV ZHM דלהיט

224: ואתתקף / ZHV ZHM [ביה]

243: גבורן / ZHM [וכולא מהני ג' גוונין דקאמרן . ע"ד כתיב מי ימלל גבורות ה' בגין]

243: מילין / ZHM כלילן

252: דשליט עלייהו / ZHM [דהא מהכא מתפרשן לתתא עד דמטו לאינון שליטין ממנן דאינון רתיכין לתתא וכלהו אשתמודעין ברזא דההוא שמא דשליט עלייהו]

261: כללא / ZHV ZHM כלילא

262: רוחא / ZHV ZHM וי

264: דסלקא ריחייא / ZHM דסלקין ריחא

267: מייא ורוחא / ZHV ZHM רוחא ומייא

276: סטרא / ZHV ZHM שמא

293-4: ומהכא . . . דמתפרשן / ZHV ZHM חסר

305: כגוונא / ZHV ZHM כגוונין

306: דאתתקף / ZHV ZHM אתתקף

326: לאתגליא / ZHV ZHM באתגליא

329: לעילא / ZHM [אוף הכי מתפרשן לתתא כגוונא דלעילא דכתיב כי מעולם המה מעולם המה לעילא]

333: הוו / ZHM [דאדכר]

## ARAMAIC TEXT

(43a) סתרי אותיות השי"ת מן הזוהר | ר"ש פתח מי ימלל
גבורות יי ישמיע כל תהלתו | מי לא ייראך מלך הגוים
כי לך יאתה כי בכל חכמי הגוים ובכל מלכותם מאין כמוך
באתוון סתימן   דמחקקן | ע"ג סתימו דסרטא דקיומא סלקן
רתיכן ברתיכן קדישין כל רתיכא ורתיכא סלקא באת רשימא   5
אתרשים את בקיומי | סליק בגויה ההוא רתיכא כל את ואת
קאים על קיומיה דההוא רתיכא דאתחזי ליה מהכא סלקא
מלה לאתפרשא | כל את ואת ברזא דרתיכין קדישין רזא
דאת קדמאה סלקא   ונחתא סליק בעטרוי לגביה   מאה עלמין
לקבל דא את | יוד סלקא ברעו דמחשבה ואסתים ולא אתידע   10
אתחפיא תחותיה חד אגוז דחפיא טמירא בטמירו ואיהי
רתיכא | דקיימ' תחות ההוא רזא טמירא וההוא את קיימא
בגניזו נקודה חדא תחותיה ההוא אגוזא קיימ' בשית
סמכין | וסמכין ליה בשית סטרין אינון שית סטרין
גניזין גו ההוא אגוזא נפקא מגו סטרא דאת דא חד רתיכא   15
קדישא | ואיהי רתיכא גניז ולא אתגליא בר כד נהיר
נהירו דההוא אגוזא טמירא כדין אתגליא ההוא רתיכא
וההוא רתיכא | טמיר וגליא ואיהי נפקא מגו נציצו
דבוצינא כד מדיד משחתא תחות קוצא קדמאה וההוא נציצו
כד משחתא | קיימא נהיר דא וסלקא ונחתא ואסתמיך תחות   20

1 מי | תהלים קו ב / 2 מי | ירמיהו י ז

1 סתרי...הזוהר | ס ק חסר. / 2 תהלתו | ק [וגו'] / 3 ובכל
...כמוך | ק וגו' / 4 סתימן | ס ק רשימן / 5 רתיכן ברתיכן
| ס ק רתיכין ברתיכין / 6 בקיומי | ס ק בקיומיה / 8 קדישין
| ס ק [בארבע סטרי עלמא] / 9 לגביה | ס ק לגבי / 11 אגוז
| ס ק אגוזא / 13 נקודה | ס נקודא / 14 ליה | ס לה ק חסר.
/ 15 גניזין | ק חסר. / גו | ס ק בגו / 16-15 נפקא...
קדישא | ק מגו סט' דאת דא נפקא תיבה חד קדישא / 17-16
כד... טמירא | ס ב"פ/ 19 דבוצינא | ס דבוסינא/ קוצא | ס ק
קשרא

## THE SECRETS OF THE LETTERS

את יוד בסטרא אחרא לבתר אתפשט ההוא נציצו ואפיק תלת
נציצין אחרנין ואסתמכאן תחות קוצא תתאה דיוד לבתר
נפקא מגו קשרא תניינא נציצו אחרא דנהיר וסלקא
ונחתא ואסתמיך תחות את יוד בסטרא אחרא לבתר אתפשט
ההוא נציצו ואפיק תלת נציצין אחרנין ואסתמכן | בסטרא   25
דא תחות את יוד לבתר נפקא מגו קשרא תליתאה נציצו
אחרא ומגו דא אתקשר רזא דחול במשחתא || (43b) דבוצינא
אשתכחו לאת יוד נקודה עילאה ט' סמכין על מה דאסתמיך
וכולהו רתיכא לגבי את דא כדין אתנהיר | ואסתמיך על
ט' סמכין אילין וכדין נהרין מגווה תמניא אחרנין   30
וכולהו קיימין ברזא דאת יוד נקודה עילאה טמירא
אילין ט' סמכין דלתתא סלקין בשמא ולא סלקין בגין
דאינון ט' דאיקרון אין סוף קיימין ולא קיימין ולא
אתידעו ואקרון | ולא איקרון ולא ידיעו כלל ואלין
סלקין בשמא ורזא לפניך וחנותי את אשר אחון ורחמתי את   35
אשר ארחם לית מאן | דיקום בהון ובשמהן דילהון ולא
אתגליא למיקם באורחייהו ועל דא לא קאים משה עלייהו
בגין דהוו מקדמת דרגא | דיליה בההוא נציצו קדמאה
כתי' לפניך וכן כולהו קיימין ואקדימו לדרגא דיליה
וכל דא לא קאים בארחוי דקב"ה בגין | דכולהו סלקין גו   40

35 לפניך | שמות לג יט

21 בסטרא אחרא | ס ק ואיהי נקודה חדא / 22 נציצין | ק
נצוצין / 27 דבוצינא | ס דבוציצא ק דבוציצא (ס"א דבוצינא)
/ 28 לאת יוד | ס לא דיוד / ט' | ס ק תשעה / על מה | ק
עלמא / 30 ט' | ס ק תשע / מגווה | ק מגוויה / 31 נקודה |
ס נקודא / 32 ט' | ס ק תשע / 33 ט' | ס ק תשע / 36 ובשמחן
| ס ק ובשמהון / 38 בההוא | ס ק דהחוא / 39 ואקדימו | ק
אקדימו

## ARAMAIC TEXT

מחשבה ומתמן מתפשטין אורחוי לכמה סטרין ברעותיה
דקב״ה דלא אתידעו כלל סלקא את דא | באילין סמכין
לעילא בטש מאן דבטש דלא ידיע ואין סוף נהיר ולא נהיר
ונחתא ולא ידיע ממאן דנהיר כד נחית | איתכלילן ביה

45 אינון סמכין ואתפשט כד אתפשט נפקא חד נהורא כליל מן
כולא ואתחפיא ביה כמאן דעייל בחד | היכלא ההוא היכלא
קיימא בתרין סטרין דלחפייא ואתגלייא לעילא ואינון
תשע סמכין נהרין בגו ההוא היכלא ואת | יוד איגניז
בגו ההוא היכלא באינון סמכין וההוא היכלא איקרי ח״א

50 זמין ולא זמין אתגליא ולא אתגליא לא | אתגליא כלל
ברזא דא קיימא את יוד וכולהו סמכין בגין דאיהי טמירא
ובה קיימא כולה לאתעטרא האי אית | ליה חמש רתיכין
דנפקן מגו ההוא נציצו דבוצינא כד סלקא לאתרה ואתכנשת
לבתר משחתא ואילין איקרו | נפלאות נ' פלאות רזא דא

55 בעא דוד מלכא למיקם על ה' רתיכין אילין כד״א גל עיני
ואביטה נפלאות מתורתך | ואילין כד נהרין וסלקין לה
לאתעטרא אתעביד חמש לנהרא גו חמש דלתתא דנפקין
מינייהו ואינחו נ' פלאות | נהרין וסלקין לה לעילא
ואתעטראן ואתקשראן גו אינון ט' סמכין אוחרנין ואינון

60 ט' סלקין לאת יוד לעילא לעילא | כד נחתין ולא ידיע

55 גל | תהלים קי״ט י״ח

43 לעילא | ס לעילא לעילא / 46-45 מן כולא | ס ק מכלא /
51 סמכין | ק סמיכין / 52 כולה | ס ק כלא / 53 דנפקן | ס
ק דנפקין | נציצו דבוצינא | ס ק נהירו דבוציצא / לאתרה |
ק לאתרא / 54 לבתר | ס ק [דעבדת] / 55 ה' | ס ק חמש /
כד״א | ס כמד״א / 57 אתעביד | ס ק אתעבידו / 58 מינייהו |
ס ק מינה / ואינחו | ס ק ואיהו / 59 ט' | ס ק תשע / 60 ט'
| ס ק תשע

## THE SECRETS OF THE LETTERS

ממאן נחתין האי ח"א אתעטראת ברזא דנו"ן דאינון חמשין
ואינון פלאות דאינון חמש | סמכין לגויה וכד אתעטרת
ואתפשטת אהדרת מרזא דנו"ן לגו רזא דח"א אתפשטו אינון
חמש סמכין לגויה לתתא | וקיימא עלייהו כדין וכד
65  אתנהרת בכולהו כדין נפקין מינה ה' נהורין אוחרנין
משתניין ולא משתניין ימינא ושמאלא | מכאן ולהלה
קיימ' מלה לאסתמכא על רזא עילאה ברזא דשמא קדישא
למיהוי סתים דא בדא ולאשתכללא רתיכא | קדישא ואילין
חמש אילין ארבע ואינון חמש לקביל ה' סמכין ואינון ד'
70  לקבל ד' סטרי עלמא וכל חד וחד אית ליה | רתיכא
בלחודוי וכולהו רתיכאן כולהו כלילן כל רתיכא ורתיכא
בנהורא חד וכל נהורא ונהורא אתכליל באינון | סמכין
וכל סמכא וסמכא אתכליל באת ח"א והאי את ח"א אתכליל
באינון ט' סמכין וכל חד וחד אתכליל באת | יוד נקודה
75  קדמאה עילאה למיהוי כולא חד מהכא אשתכחו רתיכין
דסלקין על את ח"א מתתא לעילא כ"ה | רתיכין ורזא דא
יברכוכה מתתא לעילא מאת ח"א ולעילא ט' רתיכין דקיימן
בלחודייהו בלא חושבנא עד רזא | דיוד וכולא אסתים
בגויה מכאן ולהלה רזא דשמא קדישא לאתעטרא באינון
80  רתיכין ולאתכללא דא בדא באילין | אתוון יהו"ה אר"ש

77 יברכוכה | תהלים קמה '

61 דנו"ן | ק דנ' / 62 לגויה | ס ק לגווה / אתעטרת | ס ק
אתעטרא / 63 אינון | ס ק אלין / 64 לגויה | ס ק חסר. / 65
ה' | ס ק חמש / 66 ולהלה | ס ולהלא ק ולהלאה / 69 אילין |
ס ק אינון / ח' | ס ק חמש / ד' | ס ק ארבע / 70 ד' | ס ק
ארבע / 71 רתיכאן | ס ק רתיכין / 72 ונהורא | ק חסר. / 73
וכל | ק על / 74 ט' | ס ק תשע / 75 קדמאה עילאה | ק עילאה
קדמאה / 77 יברכוכה | ק יברכו כ"ה / ט' | ס ק תשע/ דקיימן
| ס ק דקיימין/ 79 ולהלה | ס ולהלא ק ולהלא'

## ARAMAIC TEXT

קב"ה איקרי אחד דכתי' יי אלהינו יי אחד קב"ה איקרי
ראשון דכתי' אני יי ראשון קב"ה איקרי | אחרון דכתי'
ואני אחרון בריך הוא ובריך שמיה לעלם ולעלמי עלמייא
הא רזא דכתי' ואני אחרון דא ח"א | בתראה דשמא קדישא
85 רתיכא קדישא באחרון דכתי' ואת אחרונים אני הוא אחרון
ואחרונים כולהו ברזא ||(44a) חדא איתכלילו אלין
באילין רזא דהא אינון ד' ואילין ד דאינון אחרונים
כולהו קיימי בסטרא דלעילא ומסטרא דלתתא | רתיכא דא
מיכאל גבריאל רפאל אוריאל אילין אינון ד' וחדא נקדה
90 דקיימא עלייהו אינון ה' ולא איקרי ה' דא אלא ברזא |
דאלין ד' ונקודה בתראה דשרייא עלייהו ורזא דח"א דא
דלית הות וההוא נקודה דשרייא עלייהו באמצעיתא |
אתעביד וברזא דחנוך ה"י אחרא לתתא מתקשרא בהא
ח"א וכולה חד בחד וכדין איהי למבכי וסימניך אהה |
95 בגין דכל סחרנן בישא לתתא חפיא כגוונא דדלת וסחרא
לאילין ד' ולהאי נקודה וקיימא בהאי קליפה תקיפא |
לחפייא עלה וכדין איתכסיא סיהרא ונהירו דילה אתחפיא
וכדין אתיהיב רשו למידן עלמא בדינין בישין ורזא דא
ח"א | בתראה מתרוייהו בחד נקודה ה"י דהא כדין דינא
100 אתיהב ברזא דכתי' בגזרת עירין פתגמא ומימר קדישין

81 יי | דברים ו ד | 82 אני | ישעיהו מא ד / ואני | שם
מד ו / 85 ואת | שם מא ד / 94 אהה | ירמיהו א ו / 100
בגזרת | דניאל ד יד

82 יי | ק חסר. / 87 ד' (2&1) | ס ארבע / דאינון | ס ק
דאיקרון / 88 בסטרא | ס ק מסטרא / 89 ד' | ס ק ארבע/ נקדה
| ס נקודא / 90 ה' (2&1) | ס ק ח"א / 91 ד' | ס ק ארבע /
92 הות | ק הוה / 93 אתעביד | ס ק [ח"א] / ה"י | ס ק ח"א
/ לתתא | ס ק [דקיימא] / בחא | ס ק בהאי / 94 וכולה | ס ק
וכלא / 95 דכל סחרנן | ס ק דסחרנו / 96 ד' | ס ק ארבע /
קליפה | ס קליפא / 97 עלה | ק עליה / 99 ה"י | ס ק ח"א /
100 ומימר | ס ק ובמאמר

## THE SECRETS OF THE LETTERS

שאלתא | על דברת רתיכא דא קיימא בה' בתראה לא אתפרשי
דא מן דא לעלמין ובכל אתר דתשכח מיכאל דאיהו רישא
דאילין תמן איהי שכינתא כולא מתקשר דא בדא ואינון
מתקשרין גו ההיא נקודה וכולא ח״א וכד איהי חד ה״א |
105 ואת אל״ף או את יו״ד קדמאה לה ואיהי בחד נקודה כדין
איהי אתיא לאוטבא לעלמא א״ה או י״ה דהא קליפה בישא
אתברת מן קמה ולא חפיא עלה האי קיימא ברזא דא כגוונא
דא לית לך שמא קדישא באתוון רשימן דלא קיימ' | בההוא
את רתיכא דיליה בההוא שמא על מה דאסתמיך וההוא רתיכא
110 סמכא דיליה דלית לך מלכא דלא אתי | בחילוי ולא אשתכח
יחידאי ועל דא כתי' יי צבאות כולא בחדא דלא אתפרשאן
רתיכין מן שמא קדישא וכל את ואת | כליל בגויה רתיכא
דיליה וכדין כולא איהו שמא קדישא האי את ה״א אית לה
רתיכא באינון שליטין לתתא בגין דאת | ה״א איהי
115 באתגליא אבל כולהו אתוון אוחרנין אית לון רתיכא
לאתכללא באילין אתוון באילין תתאי בר האי בגין | דא
אתכליל בתתאי דלבר ואתוון אחרנין איתכללו | בהון
רתיכין קדישין דלאו אינון לכל בר כד מתחבראן היכלין
| בהיכלין תתאי בעילאי אבל לא אתכלילן באינון אתוון
120 למיהוי חד את ובגין כך כל את ואת משמא קדישא |

101 בה' | ס ק בה״א / 103 איהי | ק איהו / מתקשר | ס ק
איתקשר / 104 מתקשרין | ס מתקשראן / ההיא | ס ק ההוא /
נקודה | ס נקודא / 107 אתברת | ס אתעברת / מן קמה | ס ק
מקמה / 111 כתי' | ק חסר. / בחדא | ס ק כחדא / 114 ה״א | ס
ק דא / 115 באתגליא | ס ק [זעירא דמן חברייא] / אית | ס
ק לית / 116 באילין | ס ק באינון / בגין | ס ק [דאת] /
118 לכל | ס ק לבר

## ARAMAIC TEXT

אתכליל ביה רתיכיה בגויה ודא הוא שמא קדישא כדקא
יאות וכן לכל את ואת מאינון ד' ואינון ד' אינון רזא
דרתיכא | למאן דלא אתידע ולכל את ואת אית ליה רתיכא
ואתכליל בגויה ואתרשים בההוא את ממש האי ה"א איהי
125 תריסר | וההיא נקודה דקיימא לעילא איהי תליסר ואינון
תליסר מכילאן דרחמי לתתא כגוונא דלעילא הני מכילאן
תליסר תריסר אינון תריסר תחומין ואינון לארבע סטרי
עלמא תלת תלת לכל סטר ואינון תלת אינון תשעה | לכל
סטר לסטר מזרח תשעה לסטר מערב תשעה לסטר צפון תשעה
130 לסטר דרום תשעה והאי נקודה | דקיימא עלייהו באמצעיתא
אשתכח האי נקודה דאשתלים לכל סטר בגין דקיימ'
באמצעיתא לסטר מזרח | עשרה לסטר מערב עשרה לסטר צפון
עשרה לסטר דרום עשרה עשר ספיראן לכל סטר ואילין
אינון מ' אתוון | דקיימן דבראשית לתתא ברזא דשמא
135 קדישא ותרין אזנין לאחדא בימינא ושמאלא וכולהו
קיימין ברזא דה"א | השתא אשתכח דה"א דא בכל אילין
רזין עילאין בההוא רתיכא קדישא באינון תליסר ברזא
דעשר ספיראן | ברזא דמ"ב אתוון מחקקן דבשמא קדישא
דכולא אתכליל בהאי דיוקנא דה"א וכולהו קיימי
140 באלכסונא | ברזא דנקודה דקיימא באמצעיתא דארע

122 ד' (1&2) | ס ק ארבע / אינון | ס אתוון ק אתוון אינון
/ 123 למאן | ס למאי / 124 ואתכליל | ס ק דאתכליל / בההוא
| ס לההוא / איהי / ס איהו / 125 וההיא | ס ק והאי / 126-
127 מכילן תליסר | ס ק חסר. / 127 לארבע | ק לד' / / 130
נקודה | ס נקודא / 131 דאשתלים | ס ק דאשלים / 134 מ' | ס
ארבעין / דקיימן / ס [ברזא] ק דקיימין ברזא / 135 לאחדא |
ק לאתאחדא / 137 תליסר | ס ק תריסר / 138 דמ"ב ס דארבעין
ותרין / 139 דכולא | ק כלא / 140 דנקודה | ס דנקודא

## THE SECRETS OF THE LETTERS

לכולהו באורח מישור סטרא דא בסטרא דא וכן לארבע |
סטרין כולהו קיימין במתקלא תקלא דקיימא לאתקנא כולא
ברזא דא אתבריאו ואתתקנו כל הני תתאי ||(44b) ועל דא
כתי' ויאמר אלהים נעשה אדם בצלמנו כדמותנו נעשה ודא
145 איהי ה"א וכל הני דקיימן לתתא ואתאחידו ביה |
בדיוקנא ממש במה דאיקרי ה"א בר מה"א דאתאחידת לעילא
במה דלא יתחזי כלל בדיוקנהא ולא אתרשים בה | לאתחזהא
כד איקרי ה"א אזדמנת בכל הני רזין איהי כולא בגין דא
קיימא האי נקודה גו אמצעיתא בגין דאיהי | אחידת
150 בכולא אלין דלסטר מזרח אתאחידת בהו ואיהי עמהון
ובגין כך איהי בכולא וכולהו בה וכולא ח"א ועל דא |
כתי' נעשה אדם וכתי' ויאמר אלהים כולא איהו ברזא
עילאה כדקא חזי וכל הני רזין וכל רזין עילאין כולהו
אשתמודעאן בהני אתוון ואתרשימו בההוא את ממש |
155 לאתיחדא שמא קדישא כדקא יאות וכולא רזא עילאה | בשמא
קדישא עד הכא אתרמיזת חכמה עילאה ברזא דאת ח"א בתראה
דאתוון ד' זכאה חולקיה מאן דעאל ונפק | וידע אורחוי
דקב"ה למיעל בלא כיסופא לעלמא דאתי רזא דאת ו' רתיכא
קדישא | עילאה דקיימא בקיומא שלים האי את אתפליג
160 לתרין אתוון דאינון | תרין ווין ו"ו דא כגוונא דדא

144 ויאמר | בראשית א כו

141 לארבע | ק לד' / 143 ואתתקנו | ק ואתקנו / 145 איהי |
ס ק איהו / דקיימן | ק דקיימין / ביה | ס ק בה / 146 מה"א
| ס ק מה / 147 יתחזי | ס ק איתחזי / לאתחזהא | ס ק לאתחזאה
/ 149 נקודה | ס נקודא / דאיהי אחידת | ס ק דאתאחידת / ס
150 בכולא | ק בלבא / דלסטר | ק לסטר / 151 וכולהו | ס
וכלא / 152 איהו | ס חוא | 155 וכולא | ס [הוא] / 157 ד'
| ס ק ארבע / 158 ו' | ס ק ו"ו / 160 דדא | ק דא ו"ו

## ARAMAIC TEXT

ואינון תריסר רזין עילאין האי ו"ו עילאה איהי קיימא
בחמש סמכין עילאין | דקיימא עלייהו את ה"א עילאה
והאי ו"ו אע"ג דאיהי שית ורזא דשית איהי חמש ורזא
דחמש וכולא איהו כדקא | חזי שרותא בסטרא דימינא
165 רזא דנהורא קדמאה דא קיימ' על רתיכא חדא דאיהי תלת
תלת ולא ארבע | ואע"ג דלית רתיכא אלא בד' כולא הכא
ברזא דתלת תלת כמא דאתוון אזלין בשמא קדישא ובגין כך
כולא אזלא | בתלת תלת את ה"א איהי רביעתא דאתוון
ובגיני כך רתיכא כולא איהו בד' ואע"ג דאיהי בד' איהי
170 בתלת תלת | וכולא אזלא באורח מישר לסלקא דא כגוונא
דדא למיהוי חד רתיכא דסטר דרום דאיהו ימינא בתלתא |
דנפקא מגו בוצינא כד סלקא רוחא דנשיב בתריסר רוחין
דבוסמין דסלקין ריחא ולא סלקין כליל בתלת גוונין |
נהיר בנהירו ואשתאב בגויה חד להיט באשא וחד להיט
175 במיא וחד להיט ברוחא והאי אתפרש והוי תלת | האי רוחא
כד אתפרש והוי תלת גוונין אילין לאו אינון אשא ולאו
אינון מיא ולאו אינון רוחא אלא האי רוחא כד | אתפרש
כל חד נהיר ולהיט ויהיב תוקפא לאתר דעליה ולבתר
אתעביד סמך תחותיה גוונא חדא אתלהיט | ואתתקף ביה
180 אשא דאתכליל בהאי סטרא דימינא גוונא אחרא אתלהטו

163 אע"ג דאיהי שית | ס ב"פ / 166 בד' | ס ק באֹרבע / 168
ה"א | ס [דקאמרן] ק [דקא אמרן] / 169 ובגיני | ס ובגין /
כולא | ס ק דילה / בד' (1&2) | ס ק בארבע / 171 דסטר | ק
דלסטר / ימינא | ס ק [ההוא רתיכא] / 172 דנפקא | ס ק די
נפקא / בוצינא | ס ק בוציצא / בתריסר | ק בי"ב / 172-173
רוחין דבוסמין | ס ריחין דבוסמין ק תחומין / 176 אתפרש |
ס [כל חד וחד נהיר] / 178 חד | ס ק [וחד] / 179 חדא | ס ק
חד / ואתתקף | ק ואתקף

## THE SECRETS OF THE LETTERS

ואתתקפו מיא דאתכלילו בימינא | גוונא אחרא אתלהיט
ואתתקף ביה רוחא דאתכליל בהאי סטרא דימינא ואילין
תלת גוונין אינון רתיכא חדא | לסטר ימינא ברזא דאת
ו' ואילין אינון כינוויין דאית ביה בקב"ה ברזא דאינון
185 שמהן דאיקרי בהו ועל דא | דקב"ה איקרי בכמה שמהן
וכולהו אתכלילו בכל רזא ורזא מאינון סטרין עילאין
דאינון שמהן דלא נמחקין | סטרא דא דאיהו ימינא איקרי
אל רתיכא דיליה איקרי גדול בכללא כד אתפרשאן האי
רתיכא דאילין אינון תלת | גוונין הני אינון שמהן
190 איקרון גדול חסיד קדוש הני אינון רתיכא לימינא
דאיקרי אל רזא עילאה מאינון | שמהן עשרה כמא
דאוקימנא הני תלת גוונין דאינון רתיכא לסטר ימינא
להטין ונהרין וכל גוון וגוון מהני | תלתא אתפרש
לתרין אוחרנין לכל סטרא עד דעאלו בחושבנא תלת תלת
195 ואינון ט' והאי ימינא דעלייהו דרכיבי | משלים לעשרה
אוף נמי כל הני איקרון ספיראן עילאין וזעירין וכולהו
מדין דקב"ה תרין דנפקו מגו גוון חד | דאתתקף ביה מיא
חד איקרי רחום וחד איקרי חנון ואילין אינון מההוא
גוון דאתתקף במיא תרין דנפקו (45a)|| מההוא גוון אשא
200 חד איקרי ארך אפים וחד איקרי רב חסד אילין אינון

---

181 ואתתקפו | ס [ביה] ק ואתקפו ביה / 182 ואתתקף | ק
ואתקף / 184 ו' | ס ק ו"ו / 185 דא | ס ק [שמא] / 186
מאינון | ס ק מאלין / 189 הני | ק הכי / 190 חסיד | ס ק
חסין / 193 ונהרין | ס ק [לתתא] / 194 עד | ק על / 195
ט' | ס ק תשעה / משלים | ק אשלים / 197 דאתתקף | ק דאתקף
/ 198 חד | ס חסר. / ואילין | ס ק אלין / 199 דאתתקף |
דאתקף / גוון(2) | ס [דאתתקף ביה] ק [דאתקף ביה] /
201-200 חד...אשא | ס חסר.

## ARAMAIC TEXT

מההוא גוון    דאתתקף ביה אשא תרין דנפקו מההו'  |  גוון
דאתתקף ביה רוחא חד איקרי חסיד וחד איקרי סולח וברזא
דספרא דחנוך האי איקרי טוב והאי איקרי ישר  |  וסימניך
טוב וישר יי ומאילין    מתפרשין    נהורין    לתתא    וכולהו
205    רתיכין אילין לאילין וכולהו כנויין לבר אבל לא מתדבק
|  באילין לגבי עילא וכולהו כלילן בסטרא דימינא
וכולהו חד    לגבי האי סטרא וכולהו ברזא דאת ו' שירותא
|  בסטרא דשמאלא    רזא דחשוכא דמתפשטא בחשוכא לתתא עד
דמיתברי מניה גהינם  |  מלהטא מההוא חשוכא דאשא    תקיפא
210    סומקא אוכמא והכא מלהטין שביבין תקיפין דנגדין
ואתמשכאן לתתא    |  וכולהו מגו חשוכא דאיהו שמאלא להאי
סטרא כד    בוצינא    סלקא    מגו    מדידו דמשחתא נהיר לסטר
ימינא ומההו'  |    נהירו    נהיר לגבי חשוכא ומטון לגבי
דההוא אשא נהורין וקרבין לגבי ההוא    אשא    לגבי    ההוא
215    ימינא    ונהיר    מיניה    כדין  |  אתפשט ונהיר מגו בוציצא
רוחא אחרא    דנהיר מלהטא האי איהו אתפשט למיהוי רתיכא
לההוא סטרא    דשמאלא  |    אתפשט ברזא דתלת גוונין לגבי
האי סטרא דאיקרי צפון והאי רוחא לא סליק בבוסמין ולא
ריחא בגין דהאי שמאלא  |  אסתמיך על    ההוא רוחא דאתפרש
220    בתלת    גוונין    אילין גוונין    נהרין בתלת סטרין אילין

204 טוב  |  תהלים כה ח

201 דאתתקף  |  ק דאתקף  /  202    דאתתקף  |  ק דאתתקף  /  204
מתפרשין  |  ס ק מתפרשן  /  205 מתדבק  |  ס ק מתדבקאן  /  206
באילין  |  ס כאילין  /  207 וכולהו(2)  |  ס ק וכלא  /  ו'  |  ס
ו"י ק וי"ו  /  209 דמיתברי  |  ס ק דאתברי  /  גהינם  |  ק גיהנם
/  214    דההוא  |  ק ההוא  /  215 בוציצא  |  ק בוצינא  /  220
סטרין  |  ק ב"פ  /  אילין(2)  |  ס ק חסר.

## THE SECRETS OF THE LETTERS

דאשא דאיהו סטרא דשמאלא | אשא גוון חשוך אשא גוון
סומק אשא גוון אוכם הני תלת גוונין דאתפרשאן מההוא
רוחא דנפקא מגו בוצינא | סמכין לתרין סטרין גוונא חד
אתלהט ואתתקף אשא גוון חשוך דאיהו בסטר שמאלא גוון
225 אחרא אתלהט | ואתתקף ביה אשא גוון סומק דאיהו בסטר
שמאלא גוון תליתאה אתלהיט ואתתקף ביה אשא גוון אוכם
דאיהו | בההוא סטר שמאלא ואילין תלת גוונין אינון
רתיכא חדא לסטר שמאלא ברזא דאת ו"ו אילין איקרון
כינוויין לקב"ה | ברזא דשמאלא חד איקרי אדיר וחד
230 איקרי חזק וכולא בכללא חדא איקרי גבור בגין דסטרא דא
איקרי שמאלא | איהו אלהים ואוקימנא לכמה סטרין איקרי
אלהים הני תלת גוונין דאינון בסטר שמאלא מלהטין
נהרין | לתתא וכל גוון מהני תלתא מתפרש לתרין
אוחרנין לכל סטרא עד דעאלו בחושבנא תלת תלת אינון ט'
235 כמא | דאוקימנא בסטרא אחרא והאי שמאלא דעלייהו רכיב
אשלים לעשרה תרין דנפקו מגו גוון חד דאתכליל גוון |
חשוך חד איקרי שופט וחד איקרי דיין כד"א אלהים שופט
וכתי' אבי יתומים ודיין אלמנות אלהים במעון קדשו |
תרין דנפקו מגו גוון חד דאתכליל מגו אשא סומקא חד
240 איקרי כביר כח וחד איקרי איש מלחמה תרין דנפקו | מגו

237 אלהים | תהלים נ ו / 238 אבי | תהלים סח ו

222 סומק | ק סומקא / אוכם | ס ק אוכמא / הני | ק הכי /
דאתפרשאן | ס ק דמתפרשן / 223 בוצינא | ס ק בוציצא / 224
ואתתקף | ק ואתקף / 224-226 גוון אחרא...שמאלא | ס חסר. /
225 ואתתקף ביה | ק ואתתקף בה / 226 גוון | ס גוונא /
226-227 גוונא...שמאלא | ק חסר. / 231 איקרי(1) | ס ק
דאיקרי / ואוקימנא | ס ק והא אוקימנא / 233 נהרין | ס ק
ונהרין / גוון | ס ק [וגוון] / מתפרש | ס ק אתפרש / 234
דעאלו | ס ב"פ / אינון ט' | ס ק ואינון תשעה/ 236 דאתכליל
| ס ק [גו אשא] / 237 כד"א | ס כמד"א כי / 238 אלהים
במעון קדשו | ק וגו'

## ARAMAIC TEXT

גוון דאתכליל ואתתקף גו גוון אשא אוכמא חד איקרי
פוקד עון וחד איקרי משלם גמול ומהכא מתפרשאן | לתתא
לכמה גבורן דלית לון חושבנא וכולהו מילין בסטר שמאלא
ובכולהו איקרי קב"ה וכולהו רתיכין לתתא | ולכל סטר
245 וסטר וכולא ברזא דאת ו"ו בגין דכל את ואת מהני ד'
אתוון דברזא דשמא קדישא כולהו קיימין | על רתיכין
קדישין סמכין על מה דאסתמיכו וכולהו רשימין עלייהו
כל חד וחד כדקא חזי ליה ואילין רתיכין | אינון
כינויין לההוא שמא על מה דקיימין ועל דא מאן דאתא
250 ליחדא שמא קדישא אצטריך למנדע כל חד | וחד מאינון
שמהן דכינויין על מה קיימין ומאן איהו שמא דשליט
עלייהו ובההוא סטרא דקיימין רתיכין | וכולא ברזא
דשמא קדישא באילין אתוון ארבע דאיקרי קב"ה בהון
זכאין אינון צדיקייא דאינון אזלין | באורח מישור
255 זכאין אינון בהאי עלמא וזכאין אינון בעלמא דאתי
דקב"ה רחים לון ||(45b) שירותא בסטרא דאמצעיתא בפתחא
דמזרח דפתחא דמזרח איהי קיימא באמצעיתא נטל תרין
סטרין | לעברא לון בעברין ודשין בסטרא דא ובסטרא דא
פתחא דא איהי כלילא מכל הני דקאמרן ודא | קיימא על
260 רתיכא עילאה ואיהו רתיכא דקיימא ברזא דאת ו"ו דא

241 ואתתקף | ק ואתקף / 242 מתפרשאן | ק אתפרשן /
245 ו"ו | ס וא"ו / ד' | ס ק ארבע / 246 דברזא | ס ק
די ברזא / 249 שמא | ק [קדישא] / דאתא | ס ק דאתי /
255 אינון(1) | ס ק חסר. / וזכאין | ס ק זכאין /
אינון(2) | ס ק חסר. / 256 בפתחא | ס בפתח / 260 דא
| ס ק חסר.

## THE SECRETS OF THE LETTERS

איהו ו"ו כללא דכל חני ודא קיימא ברזא דכל שית
סטרין עילאין דא קיימא על רתיכא חדא דאיהי תלת
בימינא ושמאלא נפקא מגו בוציצא כד סלקא רוחא דנשיב
בתריסר | ריחין דבוסמי דסלקא ריחייא ולא סלקין האי
265 רוחא נהיר בנהירו ודא איהו רוחא דאיהו שלמא ואיקרי
שלמא ודא רוחא | כד אתפרש אתפרש בתלת גוונין מלהטין
אשא ומיא ורוחא כמה בימינא וכד אתפרש כל חד וחד
להיט באתריה ויהיב | תוקפא האי נהירו דאתפשט מהאי
רוחא בכל סטרא וסטרא מהני תלתא גוונא חדא להיט באשא
270 ואתקיף ליה גוונא | אחרא להיט במיא ואפיש ליה גוונא
תליתאה להיט ברוחא ונהיר ליה כארגוונא מלהטא בתרין
סטרין אילין ואילין תלת | גוונין אינון רתיכא חדא
ברזא דאת ו"ו ואיהו רזא דו"ו ואילין אינון כינויין
דאיקרון בהון קב"ה כמא דאיתמ' דקב"ה איקרי | בכל חני
275 שמהן ואילין כינויין אתכלילן ברזא דשמא קדישא דהאי
סטרא אמצעיתא איתקרי ביה וא"ג דהאי איקרי באת ו"ו |
דא נטיל כל שמהן עילאין ותתאין וכל ד' אתוון דשמא
קדישא ביה אחידן בגין דנטל לכל סטרין עילא ותתא ודא
רזא יה"ו | הכא תלי שמא דא ואיהו יהו"ח נטיל תרי
280 אתוון לעילא ונטיל חד לתתא ואיהו קאים באמצעיתא בין

## ARAMAIC TEXT

עילא ותתא ומתרין | סטרין כדקא אמרן רתיכא דיליה
איקרי נורא בכללא כדקאמרן כד אתפרש האי רתיכא דאיהו
האי רוחא ואתפרש לתלת גוונין | אחרנין דאיקרון נורא
נוצר חסד אמת הני אינון הני תלת דאינון רתיכא קדישא
285 להאי סטרא דקיימא באמצעיתא הני תלת | גוונין דאינון
רתיכא קדישא דאת ו"ו להטין ונהרין לתתא וכל גוון
מהני תלתא אתפרש לתרין אחרנין לכל סטרא עד |
דאתעבידו בחושבנא תלת תלת לכל סטרא ואינון תשעה והאי
שמא קדישא דשליט עלייהו אשלים לעשרה וכל חד וחד |
290 מהני סטרין תלתא דקאמרן ימינא ושמאלא ואמצעיתא כל חד
וחד ברזא דרתיכין דיליה אינון עשרה בגין דכולא עילא
| ותתא באשלמותא חדא אינון עשר ספיראן עשר אמירן
ובגין כך כל חד וחד מהני סטרין סלקא לעשרה ומהכא |
לחושבן סגיא בגין דמתפרשן רתיכין לכל סטר עד דסליק
295 כל חד וחד לחושבן סגיא ותא חזי כל רתיכין אילין כד
מתפרשאן | לסטרייהו כולהו איקרו בההוא שמא דשליט
עלייהו וברזא דההוא את ממש לתתא תרין דנפקו מגו
נקודה חדא חד | איקרי נושא עון וחד איקרי עובר על
פשע אילין אתוון מההוא גוון דאתתקף ביה מיא תרין
300 דנפקו מגו גוון דאתתקף | ביה אשא חד איקרי מרום וחד

281 כדקא אמרן | ס ק כדקאמרן / 282 כדקאמרן | ס ק חסר. /
283 רוחא | ס ק [כדקאמרן] / 284 נוצר חסד אמת | ס ק אמת
נוצר חסד / 291 אינון | ס ק איהו / 292 אמירן | ס ק [וכל
הני רתיכין בההוא סטרא דשליט עלייהו איקרי (אקרון ק) עשר
ספיראן עשר אמיראן] / 296 בההוא | ק בהאי / 298 נקודה | ס
נקודא / 299 אתוון | ס ק אינון / דאתתקף | ק דאתקף / 300
דאתתקף | ק דאתקף

איקרי רם וברזא דחנוך שמחאן אילין כלילאן ברזא דעלמא
דאתי והכא בחאי סטרא | בוחן לבות מרום כד"א מרום
משפטיך מנגדו וכתי' אדיר במרום יי ואע"ג דשמא דא
קאים בעלמא דאתי הא כתיב | מרום ועל דא אשתתף עלמא
דאתי בכל חני וחכי איקרי אלהים כגוונא דשמאלא וכולא     305
חד גוונא תליתאה דאתתקף | ביה רוחא אינון תרין דנפקו
מיניה חד איקרי שוכן עד וחד איקרי קדוש ומאילין
אתפרשאן נהורין לתתא וכולהו רתיכין | אילין לאילין
וכולהו כינוויין דאיקרי בהו קב"ה וכולהו אשתמודעאן
בסטרא דשליט עלייהו כגוונא דא אית סטרין תלתא |     310
דנפקין מגו אלין סטרין עילאין דקאמרן דאינון ימינא
ושמאלא ואמצעיתא ואילין נפקי לבר מינייהו ונפקי תרין
מינייהו | וכולהו נטלי רתיכין לתתא כגוונא דאילין
עילאין ולא עילאין בגינייהו ואלין דלתתא דנפקי מגו
אילין עילאין סטרין דקאמרן | אינון כגוונא דילהון חד     315
איקרי ימינא וחד איקרי שמאלא וחד דקאי באמצעיתא גו
ההוא אמצעיתא דקא אמרן וכולהו || (46a) כלילן ברזא
דאת ו"ו דכליל כולהו וכולהו ברתיכין ידיעאן דמתפרשין
בסטרייהו ואילין לא איקרו בשמהן ידיעאן בר באינון
כינוויין | דלתתא כגוונא דאינון כינוויין עילאין     320

302 מרום | תהלים י ה / 303 אדיר | תהלים צג ד

302 כד"א | ס כמד"א / 303 יי | ק [וכתיב ואדיר במרום יי]
/ 305 כגוונא | ס ק בגווני / 306 דאתתקף | ק דאתקף / 310
בסטרא | ס ק לסטרא / 312 ונפקי | ס ק וקיימין / 313
מינייהו | ס ק [לבר] / 314 ולא | ס ק ולאו | בגינייהו | ס
ק בגינייהו / 317 דקא אמרן | ס ק דקאמרן / כלילן | ס ק
[בחני תלת עלאין וכלהו כלילן] / 318 דמתפרשין | ס ק
דמתפרשאן

## ARAMAIC TEXT

ואינון תתאין אחידאן בעילאין והני תלת אחרנין כולהו
רתיכאן דלבר והא אוקימנא | ותא חזי הני תרין קיימין
אינון סמכין לבר ואינון ימינא ושמאלא ואיתקרון חסדי
דוד ואילין צבאות רתיכא דילהון תרין | דקיימין
ועבדין שליחותא בנביאי קשוט ומתמן מתפרשין עובדין    325
בעלמא לאתגליא ורזא דא דכתי' גדולים מעשה יי גדולים
| דנפקי מן גדול ואלין איקרון רחמיך רבים יי איה
חסדיך וגו זכור רחמיך יי וחסדיך וגו' ואע"ג דאוקימנא
דאינון לעילא | מעולם המה לתתא ועל דא לא איקרון
בשמהן כגוונא דאיקרון בשמהן אינון דלעילא ואינון    330
כגוונא דלעילא אבל אינון | בכללא אינון דקיימין לבר
ואינון סמכין דאוריתא דנפקין מרתיכין עילאין ואילין
הוו דוד מלכא ודא איהו דאדכר תדיר בכללא | כמא
דאוקימנא ת"ח כל הני שמהן עילאין מאינון עשרה דקאמרן
דלא נמחקין יאות הוא רתיכין אלין דילהון דאינון שמהן    335
| דאיקרון אינון כינויין אמאי נמחקין אלא רזא דא הא
איתמ' גו ספרא דרב המנונא סבא דכל הני שמהן עלאין
אינון קיימי | כנשמתא בגופא לנשמתא עילאה דלא אתידע
ולא אתגליא ואילין כינויין אינון לבושא לגופא כגוונא
דאגוזא דאית קליפה | לקליפה או אילין לבלבן דאית לון    340

326 גדולים | תהלים קי"א ב / 327 רחמיך | שם קי"ט קנו
/ איה | שם פט נ / 328 זכור | שם כה ו

321 ואינון | ס ק ואלין / תלת | ס ק תלתא / 323
ואיתקרון | ס ק ואיקרי / 327-328 איה חסדיך וגו | ס
חסר. ק איה חסדיך / 328 וגו(2) | ס ק כי מעולם המה /
333 איהו דאדכר תדיר | ס הוא דאידכר תמיד / 338
כנשמתא בגופא | ס ק כגופא

## THE SECRETS OF THE LETTERS

קליפה לקליפה ומוחא לגו הכי נמי כל אילין עשרה שמהן
כולהו כגוונא דההיא קליפה | למוחא ואע"ג דכולהו מוחא
וכולהו נהורין עילאין ובוסמין עילאין לית מאן דקאים
בקיומייהו אבל כולהו כגוונא דקליפה | לגבי מה דלא
345 ידיע ולא קיימא בחכמתא כלל כ"ש רזא דאין סוף והני
כינויין אינון קליפה לגבייהו וכולא דא לגו מן דא
ומוחא | סתימאה לגו בגו דלא אתידע כלל ועל דא קליפה
בתראה לא איכפת לן ואע"ג דנמחקין עם כל דא לא אתיהב
רשותא למחקא | אפי' את זעירא דאורייתא ואי תימא אי
350 הכי האי ה"א בתראה דקאמרן איהי קליפה בתראה לגבי
אילין לאו הכי קליפה איהי | לגבי אילין עילאין אבל
לגבי אינון כינויין לא דהא לא משמשין בה אלא אינון
שמהן עילאין ולא אינון כינויין אלא כד איהי | סלקא
לאתעטרא לעילא ולאתאחדא ברזא דימינא ושמאלא כל הני
355 רתיכין דאינון אינון כינויין כולהו סחרין ליה וחפיין
עלה | סחרנהא כבעלה לאתתא דפריש גדפיה עלה הכי אינון
פרשין דגדפין דבעלה עלה וחפיין לה בכל סטר ואיהי
משמשא | בבעלה וסימנא דא ואפרוש כנפי עליך ופרשת
כנפיך על אמתך ובגין כך אינון לבר ואיהי לגו ואיהי
360 לבר ואיהי לגו והני | כינויין אינון לגו ואינון לבר

358 ואפרוש | יחזקאל טז ח / ופרשת | רות ג ט

341 לגו | ס לאו הכי | כל | ס ק דא / 342 דההיא | ס דההוא
ק דהאי / ואע"ג | ס ק אע"ג / 343 וכולהו | ס ק כולהו /
344 לגבי | ס לגביה / 347 דלא | ס ולא / אתידע | ס ק ידיע
/ 352 לא(1) | ק לאו / 353 ולא | ס ק ולאו / 354 לעילא |
ס ק בעילא / ולאתאחדא | ס ולאתיחדא | 355 ליה | ס ק לה
356 סחרנהא | ס ק סחרנה / גדפיה | ס גדפה ק גדפא / 357
דבעלה | ס בעלה / 358 דא | ס חסר. / 359 איהי(1,2) | ק
איהו / 360 ואיהי | ק איהו

## ARAMAIC TEXT

מה דאיהו לגו קיימא לבר מה דאיהו לבר קיימא לגו
וכולא שפיר איהו זכאה חולקהון | דאינון דידעי למיזל
באורח מישר דלא יטעון לא לימינא ולא לשמאלא כמא
דאוקימנא כי ישרים דרכי יי וצדיקים ילכו בם |
365 ופושעים יכשלו בם מבועא דבירא דלא פסיק לעלמין האי
קיימא קיומא לקיימא כולה כולהו עילאין וכולהו תתאין
| קיימאן בהא לרחמא דתיאובתה בגין דאיהו קיומא לעילא
ותתא לאנהרא אנפין ולאשקאה גנתא בהאי לאו רתיכא |
קיימא ביה לאתגליא אלא כולא סתים בסתימו ולא קיימא
370 באתגליא אלא כולהו שמהן עילאין וכולהו רתיכין כולהו
אתייאן | לגביה בלחישו כד אינון שמהן אתיין לגביה
אילין רתיכין פרישאן וחפיין לכל סטרין לדרגא דא
ולדרגא דלתתא ואילין איקרון | גדפין דבעלה לחפייא על
כולא והאי דרגא עאל בלחישו במבועא גו בירא דלא פסקין
375 מימוי לעלמין ולא אתפרש מבועא | לעלמין וכולא איהו
באר דכתי' באר חפרוה שרים מים חיים והא אוקימנא האי
מבועא דבירא איהו סתים לגבי ההוא | בירא דעאל לגביה
בלחישו והאי כרי גו חחוא נקודח דקאמרן רזא דהא בתראה
וכרי בה ועאל לגבה ולא אתידע כלל והאי | איהו כמא
380 דאוקימנא דכד אל"ף אתחבר בה"א או יו"ד ההיא ח"א

364 כי | הושע יד י' / 376 באר | במדבר כא יח (שה"ש ד
טו)

363 לא לימינא ולא לשמאלא | ס ק לימינא ולשמאלא /
366 כולא | ס ק כלא / 367 קיימאן | ק קיימין /
דתיאובתה | ס ק דתיאובתא / קיומא | ס תיובתא ק
תיאובתא / 369 כולא | ס ק [איהי] / 371 אתייאן | ס ק
אתאן | כד | ק בר / 374 עאל | ס על / במבועא | ס
כמבועא / 377 דעאל | ס דעל / 378 כרי | ק קארי / 379
וכרי | ק וקרי / והאי | ס והא / 380 ההיא | ק האי

171

## THE SECRETS OF THE LETTERS

איהי כנקודה חדא לאוטבא לעלמא כגון א"ח או י"ח כדין
(46b)|| ההוא מבועא דבירא גו ההוא נקודה ועאל לגוה
ולא אתידע וכדין ההיא נקודה קיימא ברזא דקדש הקדשים
ועל דא רזא | דדוכרנה דילה איהו ברזא דקדש הקדשים
385 דמפקנו דרוחא קיימא בבי גרונא א"ח י"ח בגין דהא איהו
אתר דקיימא קדש | הקדשים קול גדול ולא אשתמע ולאו
איהו רוח וכדין איהו ח"א בחבורא דאינון אתוון עילאין
וכולא שמא חדא לאנהרא מעילא | ותתא כד כרי האי מבועא
בהאי נקודה ועאל בגוה כדין כל אינון שמהן עילאין וכל
390 אינון סטרין עילאין דקא אמרן כולהו | עאלין בגוון
כתיובתא ברוחא שלים לעילא בתיאובתא עאלין בה ולא
במלה אחרא כולה ברוחא ולא בגופא דאשתליל מכל |
לבושוי בשעתא דאתי לאזדווגא באתתיה הכי נמי כל אינון
רתיכין דקאמרן דעילא ותתא כולהו סחרין לה ואינון
395 חפיין עלה | ובעלה אשתליל מכולהו ועל דא לא אתיין כל
אינון שייפין לאתחברא בה אלא ברוחא ממש וכדין כולה
איהו רעותא חדא | ועל דא בשעתה דקב"ה זמין לגבה
וישראל לאו אינון זכאין דאינון פתילה לאנהרא מה כתי'
פשטתי את כתנתי איככה | אלבשנה רחצתי את רגלי איככה
400 אטנפם פשטתי את כתנתי אילין אינון כינויין דקאמראן

399 פשטתי | שה"ש ה ג

381 כנקודה | ס ק בנקודה / 382 לגוה | ק לגבה / 384
דדוכרנה | ס ק דדוכרנא / איהו ס ק איהי / 385 דהא | ק
דהאי / 386 אשתמע | ק אשתמודע / 387 רוח | ס ק [ממש]
/ 388 ותתא | ס ק ומתתא / כרי | ק ברי / 389 ועאל | ס ועל /
389-390 וכל...עילאין | ק חסר. / 390 דקא אמרן | ס ק
דקאמרן / בגוון | ס בגווה ק לגווה / 391 כתיובתא | ס ק
בתיאובתא / 392 כולה | ס ק כלא / בגופא | ס ק [כבעלה] /
394 דעילא | ס דלעילא / סחרין | ק סחרנין / 396 כולה | ס
כלא ק כד / 397 בשעתה | ס ק בשעתא

## ARAMAIC TEXT

דכולהו כד מתחבראן אילין אינון | כיתונא דקב"ה וכד
איהו זמין לגבה אשתליל מכולהו לאתחברא בהדה ועל דא
פשטתי את כתנתי לאתקנא ולמהוי זמין | לאוטבא לך ואת
לא מתתקנא כדקא יאות השתא איככה אלבשנה ואתהדר
ואסתלק מינה רחצתי את רגלי איככה אטנפם | הא אסחית 405
רגלי מההוא טנופא ומאי איהו בגין דכד אתתקנית
ואזדמנית לגבך אעברית ההוא סטרא אחרא מסאבא | מקמי
רגלי השתא אכדין אהדר לשואה ההוא טינופייא לחפייא על
מקדשא הואיל ואת לא זמינת בתיקונך לאתתקנא | לגבי
הכא אולפנא דכד רוח מסאבא אתעבר מעלמא כדין אתדכי 410
כולא עילא ותתא ועל דא רחצתי את רגלי איככה | אטנפם
כמלקדמין ובגין כך כל אינון כינויין אתפשטו בשעתא
דהאי מבועא כרי בההיא נקדה ואסתים בגווה וכדין | כד
ההוא מבועא אסתים בגויה כדין כולא אנהיר ובירא
אתמליא מההוא מבועא דעאל בגויה ואסתים ביה בחשאי וכל 415
אינון | כינויין חפיין עלה ואתפשטו לסטרא דא ולסטרא
דא והכי אינון גלידין דאגוזא קלישא דקיימ' לגו וחפיא
על מוחא | וההוא קליפה תקיפא אתברת ולא קיימ' תמן
וכדין כולא איהו ברזא עילאה למהך ברזין אילין זכאין
אילין דמסתכלין | ברעותא דמארייהו ברזין דמלין אילין 420

401 אילין | ס ק חסר. / כיתונא | ק כתננא / 402 לגבה | ס
[איהו] ק לגביה איהו / 403 את כתנתי | ק חסר. / לך | ק
חסר. / 404 מתתקנא | ק מתקנ' / 406 אתתקנית | ס אתתקנת ק
אתקנת / 408 לשואה | ס ק לשויא / טינופייא | ס ק טינופא
לחפייא | ס ק לחפאה / 409 לאתתקנא | ק לאתקנא / לגבי | ס
ק לגבאי / 410 אתדכי | ק אתרבי / 411 כולא | ס חסר. / דא
| ס חסר. / 413 כרי | ק ברי / בההיא | ס ק בההוא | בגווה
| ס ק בגויה / 414-413 וכדין...בגויה | ק חסר. / 417 והכי
| ס ק והני / לגו וחפייא | ס ק וחפייא לגו / 419 איהו | ק
איהי / 420 אילין(1) | ס ק אינון / ברעותא...אילין | ס ק
ברעותייהו מילין דרזין

## THE SECRETS OF THE LETTERS

עילאין למהך באורח קשוט למיזכי בהאי עלמא ולאנהרא
לון לעלמא דאתי עלייהו | כתי' והמשכילים יזהירו
כזוהר הרקיע וגו' זכאין אינון בעלמא דין ובעלמא
דאתי דיוקנא דאתוון ברזא קדישא ה"א תתאה | דקאמרן

425 רזא דמקדשא סיחרא כד שלטא ואתקדשת לגבי שמשא לקבלה
נהורא מיניה אינון קיימין כתרין רחימין דא לקבל | דא
ואנין עולימתאן דקיימן בהדא אתפשטן ואתתקנת בתיקונין
חדא בתראה וחדא לקמה וחדא מסטרא דא וחדא | מסטרא דא
ואיהי קיימא באמצעיתא וע"ב סנהדרין קיימין בפלגו

430 גורן עגולה למעבד גופא לסהרא לאתקשטא מטרונית | לגבי
בעלה ואיהי קיימא כגוונא דא ◯ בפלגו סיהרא ודא נקדה
באמצעיתא דההיא נקדה נטלא נהורא מן שמשא | לאנהרא
לכל גופא ורזא דא נקדה דקיימ' בפלגו דעינא כולה
קיימ' בההיא נקודה דקיימ' באמצעיתא | דאיהי נטלא כל

435 נהורא לאנהרא לכל עינא וסיהרא לא אנהירת אלא מגו חד
נקודה דקיימ' ואסתים גו אמצעיתא אע"ג דלא | אתחזיא
בסיהרא ת"ח לית לך עגולה בעלמא דלא אתעביד מגו נקודה
חדא דקיימ' באמצעיתא ובגין כך עיגולא | דסיהרא מגו
חד נקודה דאסתים בגווה באמצעיתא אתעביד כולא והחיא

440 נקדה דקיימ' באמצעיתא נטיל כל נהורא | ואנהיר לה

422 והמשכילים | דניאל יב ג

422 לעלמא | ס ק בעלמא | 423 וגו' | ס ק ומצדיקי הרבים
ככוכבים לעולם ועד | 425 ואתקדשת | ס ק ואתקשטת / לקבלה |
ס ק לקבלא | 427 ואנין עולימתאן / ס ק ואינון בתולתאן
דקיימן | ק דקיימין / בהדא | ס ק בהדה / אתפשטן | ס ק
אתקשטן / ואתתקנת | ס ואתתקנן ק ואתקנן / 428 בתראה | ס ק
בתרחא / לקמה | ק לקמהא / 429 וע"ב | ס ק ושבעין ותרין /
430 מטרונית | ס ק מטרוניתא / 431 בפלגו | ס ק כפלגו /
433 כולה | ס ק כלא / 434 בההיא | ס ק בחהוא / נטלה | ס
נטלא / 437 בסיהרא | ס כסיהרא / עגולה | ס ק עגולא /
נקודה | ס נקודא / 439 נקודה | ס נקודא / והחיא | ק והאי

## ARAMAIC TEXT

לגופא ואתנהיר כולא רזא דרזין לאינון דמסתכלין ברזי
דחכמתא האי ה"א דאיהו פלגו דגופא דסיהרא ‖(47a)
ואיהי בעגולה כדקא אמרן בגו ההיא נקודה דקיימא גו
גו אמצעיתא אמאי איהו פלגו לאו פלגו אלא סתימה מסטרא
445 דא ｜ ופתיחא מסטרא דא כנוקבא דפתיחא לגבי דכורא
לקבלה ליה ובג"ד איקרי ה"א מאי ה"א כמ"ד הא אנא וכד
איהי אתנהירת ｜ מיניה ואתחברו דא בדא וסהרא אתמליא
כדין האי ה"א אשתלים ואתמליא סיהרא מכולא ומאתרה
דאיהי ה"א פלגו דסיהר' ｜ אתעביד ס סהרא בשלימו
450 וקיימא כגוונא דאמא עילאה דאיהי ס סתימא כמא
דאוקימנא ברזא דמ' למרבה המשרה בס' סתימא ｜ והשתא
קיימא סיהרא באשלמותא עלמא תתאה כגוונא דעלמא עילאה
ודא איהו רזא דאת ס' ות"ח את דא את ס' לאו ｜ איהי
אלא בעגולא כיון דקיימא סיהרא באשלמותא וכולא מרזא
455 דאת ה"א כמא דאתמ' ועל דא איהי בקדמיתא פתיחא ｜ ברזא
דה"א לקבלה לבעלה ולבתר דאשתלים מיניה אתמליא
באשלמותא ואתעביד ס' כגוונא עילאה דעלמא דאתי כדקא
אמרן ובג"ד ה"א עילאה ה"א תתאה ס' עילאה ס' תתאה
כולא דא כגוונא דדא ודא איהו רזא חדא עילא ותתא כחדא
460 ת"ח ｜ עלמא עילאה איהו פתיחא בקדמיתא ברזא דה"א וכד

443 בעגולה ｜ ס בעגולא ק כעגולא/ כדקא אמרן ｜ ס ק כדקאמרן
/ ההיא ｜ ק ההוא / 449 ה"א ｜ ק ה' / 444 גו ｜ ס ק חסר. /
446 לקבלה ｜ ס ק לקבלא/ ליה / ס ק [בגווה ולאתנהרא מיניה /
ולאתחברא בהדיה ועל דא איהי פתיחא לגביה לקבלא ליה] /
ובג"ד ｜ ס ק כדין / כמ"ד ｜ ס ק כמאן דאמ' / 448 ומאתרה ｜
ס ק ומאת דא / 451 דמ'...סתימא ｜ ס סרבה המשרה ק לסרבה
המשרה/ 452 באשלמותא עלמא ｜ ס באשלמותא עלמה 453 את ｜ ס
ק חסר. / 454 בעגולא ｜ ס בעגולה/ 456 לקבלה ｜ ס ק לקבלא /
457 באשלמותא ｜ ס באשלמותה / ס' ｜ ס ס' / 457-458 כדקא
אמרן ｜ ס ק כדקאמרן / 458 ס'(1&2) ｜ ס ק ס' / 459 דדא ｜ ס
ק דא / 460 איהו ｜ ס ק איהי

## THE SECRETS OF THE LETTERS

אתמליא מאינון שבילין עילאין ואתנהרא לאנהרא אתפשטא
ואשתלים ואתעביד ס' וכולא ברזא חד דיוקנא דאת ו' |
ברזא קדישא האי את עלמא דלעילא פשיט פשיטו לאנהרא
לתתא | וההוא פשיטו איהו בשית סטרין כלילן כחדא
465 בחיבורא חדא דא כגוונא דדא ודא כגוונא דדא וכולהו
מתחבראן באינון רתיכין | כולהון באת דא האי את איהו
רשימו בשית סטרין כלילן כחדא ודא איהו דאנהיר לסיהרא
ברזא דשית סטרין כלילן דהא כד | מתחבראן כחדא פשיטין
מפשיטו כולא דיוקנא דו"ו דיוקנא דאדם ואפי' דאינון
470 בשית סטרין לא אתחזו בפשיטו בר חד גופא | רזא דרזין
לאינון דמסתכלין באורח מישור בדיוקנין דאתוון הכא
בהאי את כולהו בחיבורא חדא לאחזאה דכולהו קיימין |
בקיומא דגופא דאיהו נטיל כולא וכד האי ו"ו קיימא
הכי בחיבורא חדא האי איהו זמין לגבי נוקבא פשיט
475 ואשתליל מכולא | רזא דיוקנא דגופא דיוקנא דאדם וכד
מסתכלאן רזין דרועין מסטרא דא ומסטרא דא מתחברן בהני
גופא דלא אתחזו בר | גופא בלחודוי בגין דכולהו כלילן
ביה אימתי אתחזון בשעתא דאת דא אתפשטת ואיקרי אל"ף
כדין תרין דרועין דא מסטרא | דא ודא מסטרא דא וגופא
480 קיימ' ביינייהו באמצעיתא ועל דא אל"ף רישא לכל אתוון

---

461 אתפשטא | ס ק אתפשטת / 462 ו' | ס ק ו"ו / 463 פשיטו
| ס פשיטא / 465 חדא | ק חסר. / 466 כולהון | ס ק דילהון
/ באת | ק כאת / איהו | ס ק איהי / 467 איהו | ס ק הוא |
469 מפשיטו | ס ק בפשיטו / 470 בשית | ס ק שית / בפשיטו |
ק חסר. / 471-472 באורח...בחיבורא | ס ב"פ / 472 בחיבורא
| ק כחיבורא / קיימין | ס ק קיימן / 473 האי | ס ק ]את
דאיהו[ / 475 דיוקנא | ס ק דדיוקנא

## ARAMAIC TEXT

בגין דתיקונא דא כד קאים איהו רישא לכל | מה דנפיק
מעלמ' דאתי ואע"ג דרזין אוחרנין נאמרו ברזא דאלף אבל
דא איהו ברירו דרזא דמלה כמא דאיהו בספרא דאדם |
והכי איהו ומהכא אתפשטו אתוון אוחרנין כולהו
בסטרייהו כל חד וחד כדקא חזי ליה ואת דא כולא איהו       485
חד וא"ו ואל"ף | דהאי אסתים כולא בגויה והאי אחזי כל
דיוקניה ואי תימא תרין ירכין דלא אתחזיין הכי הוא
ודאי דהא תלת סטרין אינון | רזא דתלת אוחרנין ותו
אילין אינון רזי דתורה שבכתב ביה כללא דכולא מהכא
נפקן כל שאר כגוונא דא נביאים וכתובים כולהו | כחדא       490
דאינון אבהן וכד אבהן מתחבראן כחדא אינון חד ועל דא
איקרי אל"ף חד ריש לכל אתוון רזא דתורה שבכתב כמא |
דאיתמ' ועל דא ו"ו ואלף חדא רזא אינון את ו"ו דיוקנא
דאדם רישא וגופא אתפשוטט' חד אלף אשלמותא דדיוקנא
לאחזאה | וכי תימא ו"ו דאיהו אתפשטותא חדא פשיטו חד       495
בלא דיוקנין אוחרנין אמאי רזא דיליה שית אלף דאיהי
תלת דיוקנין אמאי | רזא דיליה חד אלא מהכא רזא
דסלקין בשמא קדישא אסיר לאסגאה לון בפרטא אלא לחברא
לון כולהו וליחדא לון כחדא | למיהוי חד וכד איהו
כחדא כללא חדא בדיוקנא חדא אית לפרשא לון ולמעבד       500

482 דרזין | ק [עלאין] / 483 איהו | ס הוא / 484 איהו | ס
ק הוא / 486 וא"ו | ס ק ו"ו / ואל"ף | ס ק [בר] / 489 רזי
| ס ק רזא / ביה | ק חסר. / מהכא | ס ק ומהכא / 490 כחדא
| ס ק [אלף איהו חד רזא דתלת גוונין כחדא] / 492 ריש | ק
רישא / 493 חדא רזא | ס ק רזא חדא / 494 אתפשוטט' | ס ק
אתפשטותא / 495 חדא | ק חד / 496 דאיהי | ס ק דאיהו / 497
רזא | ס ק רזין / 499 לון(1) | ס ק חסר. / וליחדא | ס
וליחדאה / 499-500 איהו כחדא | ס ק אינון / 500 כללא | ק
בכללא

## THE SECRETS OF THE LETTERS

פרטין דנפקין   מההוא כללא דאתחזי   ועל דא |   כלל אתחדר
למהוי פרט   פרט   אתחדר למיהוי כלל כלל דא ו"ו דאתחדר
למיהוי פרט   ברזא דשית ואיהו פשיטו חד בלחודוי |   פרט
א' תלת דיוקנין   מתחבראן   כחדא   ואתחדר למיהוי כללא
505   ברזא   דחד ורזא דא כלל ופרט וכלל א' ו' וכולא חד אלף
פרט ואתחדר   |(ב47)   למיהוי כלל כמא דאוקימנא ולבתר
אתחדר למיהוי   פרט ואיהו הוא כלל ופרט וכלל ו"ו כללא
ואתחדר למיהוי   פרט ולבתר אתחדר |   למיהוי כלל רזא דא
כלל   ופרט וכלל אל"ף   פרט   ואתחדר   למיהוי כלל כמא
510 דאוקימנא   ולבתר   אתחדר למיהוי פרט בגין דאיהו אלף |
והכי סלקא   ברזא   דאלף   דרועין   וגופא ואתפרשין רזין
למאה וממאה   לאלף   ועל   דא אלף ברזא דאלף חד כלל אלף
אלפא פרט |   ו"ו כלל ואתחדר למיהוי פרט כמא דאוקימנא
ולבתר אתחדר למיהוי כלל רזא דאדם   חד   רזא   חד וכולא
515   סלקא   ברזא   חדא |   ובמתקלא חדא למיהוי כולא חד ו"ו
אתחדר למיהוי   כולא   חד   נהורא חדא כלילא בשית סטרין
ורזא דא   וירא   אלהים   את |   האור כי טוב דא ו"ו דהוה
אזיל ונהיר ברזא דימינא בכללא חדא ולבתר ויבדל אלהים
בין האור ובין החשך אתחדר את |   דא   למיהוי   אלף תרין
520   דרועין   דא מסטרא דא ודא מסטרא דא חד איתקרי אור וחד

517 וירא | בראשית א ד

501 דאתחזי | ס דאתחדר / 504 א' | ס ק אל"ף / מתחבראן | ס
מתחברין / כללא | ס ק כלל / 505 א' ו' | ס ק א"ו ו"א /
506 כמא דאוקימנא | ס ק חסר. / 507 פרט | ק כלל ופרט /
509-507 ו"ו...| וכלל | ס חסר. ק ו"ו כלל ואתחדר' למהוי' כלל
דא רזא כלל ופרט וכלל / 511 ואתפרשין | ס ק ואתפרש / 512
דא | ס ק [איקרי] / דאלף | ס ק [אלף] / 516 כלילא | ק
כלילן / 517 דהוה | ק דהוא

## ARAMAIC TEXT

איתקרי חשך אתפליג את ו"ו בגינייהו | וכדין אתפרש
מחלוקת מתרין סטרין דאינון אור וחשך דכתי' ויבדל
אלהים בין האור ובין החשך ומהו ויבדל דאפרש מחלוקי' |
ההוא ואסתכמו תרין סטרין כחדא למיהוי בשלם והבדלה דא
525 איהי הבדלת מחלוקת לאסתכמא למיהוי כולא חד שלים כחדא
| ובגיני כך א"ו כחדא אינון ויקרא אלהים לאור יום דא
סטרא חדא דרזא דאלף לבתר אתפרישו תרין | סטרין למעבד
עובדא חד עביד ערב וחד עביד בקר כיון דעבדין עובדין
אסתכמו | תרוייהו ואתכליל באת ו"ו הה"ד ויהי ערב
530 ויהי בקר ויהי ערב מסטרא דחשך ויהי בקר מסטרא דאור
כיון דעבדו עובדין | מן יד אשתכללו בחד דכתי' ויהי
ערב ויהי בקר יום אחד דא רזא דאת ו"ו דאתכלילו ביה
למיהוי דא רזא דכתי' ויהי ולא | כתי' והיה ויהי כד
אתחזון ברזא דאלף ועבדו עובדין ואסתימו ולא אתחזון
535 כדין כתי' ויהי הוה והשתא לאו איהו דהא | אתכליל
ברזא דו"ו והשתא כולא יום אחד מי ימלל גבורות יי
ישמיע כל תהלתו ויאמר אלהים יקוו המים | מתחת השמים
אל מקום אחד יקוו המים מתחת השמים סטרא תתאה דא סטרא
חדא דברזא דאלף | דאיהו סטרא דאיקרי חשך ודא איהו
540 מתחת השמים דהא מההוא סטרא מתפרשין מיין ונבעין

526 ויקרא | בראשית א ה / 536 מי | תהלים קו ב / 537
ויאמר | בראשית א ט

521 ו"ו | ק | דא / בגינייהו | ס ק בגווייהו / אתפרש | ק
אתפלג / 523 ומהו | ס ק מהו / דאפרש | ס ק דאתפרש / 524
כחדא | ס ק חסר. / 525 איהי / ס ק היא / 528 דעבדין | ס ק
דעבדו / 529 אסתכמו | ק אסתמו / ואתכליל | ק ואתכלילו /
ו"ו | ס | י' / 531 מן יד | ס ק מיד | ס ק / 531-532 ויהי ערב
ויהי בקר | ס ק חסר. / 533 למיהוי | ס ק [חד] / ודא | ס ק
[הוא] / 534 אתחזון | אתחזיון | ס אתחזיון ק אתחזיין / 538 מקום
אחד | ק וגו' / סטרא תתאה דא | ס ק דא סטרא תתאה / 539
חדא | ק חד / דאיהו | ס ק דאיהי / איהו / ס הוא / 540
מתפרשין | ק מתפרשן

## THE SECRETS OF THE LETTERS

בנגידו בטמירו    מסטר'  |  אחרא דלעילא דאיהו ימינא אור
דאתגניז באן    אתר אתגניז ברזא דאת ו"ו וכד איהי
אתגניז כולא אתגניז סטרא אחרא  |  גניז עמיה ועל דא
מתחת השמים אל מקום אחד דא הוא דאשתאר   חד בלא חבריה
545   כד    אתגניז בקדמיתא    ומחהוא  |  סטרא כד אתפלגו מייא
ואתגניזו בגויה כדין אתחזי יבשתא מהחוא סטרא ורזא דא
הר ציון ירכתי צפון קרית מלך  |  דהא מהחוא סטרא אתחזי
ואתגליא לבתר    דאתגניזו אילין תרין סטרין אתהדר כולא
למיהוי ו"ו ואסתים כולא לגויה  |  והוה חד ויאמר אלהים
550   יהי    מארת ברקיע השמים רקיע השמים כאן ו"ו דאיהי את
דאיתקרי  |  שמים    רקיע    השמים דאתפשט מיניה פשיטו חד
לאנהרא לארעא    ולאשקא'  |  לההוא יבשתא והאי איהו רקיע
השמים מאן איהו רקיע השמים דא איהו פשיטו דאתפשט מאת
ו"ו כגוונא דא גימ"ל דא  |  איהו פשיטו דאתפשט מאת ו"ו
555   לאנהרא    ולאשקאה    לארעא כמא דאיתמר את ו"ו דיוקנא דא
אשתליל מכולא    דלא אתחזון  |  ביה כלל מכל אינון סטרין
אוחרנין בר   חד    פשיטו דגופא בלחודוי בלא דרועין
וסמכין וקיימא חכי    ברזא    דשמא קדישא  |  בגין למיהוי
זמין לגבי נוקבא לתתא    ואע"ג    דאינון    סטרין אוחרנין
560   אתרשימו לגביה    הכא רזא דרזין    לאינון  דידעי רזי  |

547 חר  |  תחלים מח ג  /  549 ויאמר  |  בראשית א יד

544 דא  |  ק ודא  /  הוא  |  ס ק [סטר'  |  546  /  ואתגניזו  |
ס ק    ואתכנישו  /  547 מלך  |  ס ק [רב]  /  549 לגויה  |  ס
ק בגויה  /  550    את  |  ס חסר.  /  551 דאיתקרי  |  ס ק
דאיקרי  /  553    איהו(2)  |  ס ק הוא  /  559 דאינון  |  ס ק
דאלין

## ARAMAIC TEXT

דמהימנותא למנדע באן זמנא איהו אלף ולאן זמנא איהו
ו' בזמנא דקיימי רזי מהימנותא ולאלפא ייחודא ברזא
דשמא | קדישא לכל עלמא כדין קיימא ברזא דאלף לעיינא
דדא ראשיתה דכולא למילף מהימנותא דייחודא דייחודא
565 דקב"ה ועל דא ||(48a) קיימא ריש לכל אתוון דהא לא
אתא בר נש לעלמא אלא למילף ולמנדע למאריה וקיימא
בדיוקנא לעיניהון דכולא אוליף | חכמתא דמהימנותא
דמארך ולמקצה השמים ועד קצה השמים ועל דא אתרשים
לגביה דבראשית בדיוקנין דאתחזי | למשאל ולמנדע דכתי'
570 כי שאל נא לימים ראשונים ודא איהי שאלתא קמייתא
לאשתמודעא בר נש למאריה דהא איהו | ראשיתה דכולא
וכדין איהו רזא דאלף ראשיתא דקיימא-לכל אתוון ובזמנא
דקיימא לאזדווגא לגבי נוקבא ברזא דשמא | קדישא קיימא
אשתלים מכולא ולא אתחזי בר גופא בלחודוי וכולא אתקשר
575 בנוקבא ב' דרועין חד תחות רישא וחד | דמחבקאן לה ועל
דא לא אתחזון באת ו"ו ירכין וההוא רקיעא כולא אסתים
בסתימו רזא דרזין ואתחזי ו"ו בלחודוי | כמאן דאשתליל
מכולא וכדין איהו זמין ואתקשר לגבה דנוקבא ועל דא
זמין את ו"ו ברזא דשמא קדישא לאחזאה כולא | לא קיימא
580 ה"א בתראה אלא שלימא ומליא כמא דאתחזי זכאה איהו

568 ולמקצה | דברים ד לב / 570 כי | שם

562-561 למנדע..מהימנותא | ס חסר. / 561 ולאן | ק וכאן /
562 ו' | ק ו"ו / בזמנא דקיימי | ק ברזא דקיימא / 562-563
ברזא..קיימא | ק ב"פ / 564 ראשיתה | ס ק ראשיתא / דכולא
| ק [למיהב] | מהימנותא דייחודא | ס יחודא דמהימנותא /
דייחודא (2) | ס ק חסר. / 569 לגביה | ס ק גביה/ 570 איהי
| ס ק איהו / 571 דהא | ס ק דדא / איהו | ס הוא / ראשיתה
| ס ק ראשיתא / 572 ובזמנא | ס בזמנא / 574 אשתלים | ס ק
אשתליל / 575 ב' דרועין | ס דרועין ק דרועא / רישא | ס ק
רישה ק רישיה / דמחבקאן | ק דמתחבקא / 576 אסתים | ס ק
[בגויה] / 577 רזא | ס ק דרזא / ואתחזי | ס ק ואתחזי

## THE SECRETS OF THE LETTERS

חולקיה דמאן  דעאל ונפק וידע בשבילין ואורחין | ברזא
דמהימנותא לאשתמודעא למאריה זכאה איהו בעלמא דין
ובעלמא דאתי  דיוקנא  דאת  יו"ד נקודה | קדמאה דסלקא
במחשבה  ואסתים  ולא  ידיע  האי  נקודה קיימא בסתימו
585   דמחשבה בגין דלא אתפשט כלל ולא ידיע | לאן אורחא הוא
ולאן אזל  ומאי  איהי  ומאי  נפקא ועל דא כולהו קיימין
בה בחהיא  נקודה  ברעו דמחשבה דלא אתידע | כלל ואיהי
נקודה דקיימא באת ה"י  קדמאה  עילאה  דקיימ' על כל
אינון שית סמכין דקאמרן ואינון חמש כדקאמרן | ואינון
590  פלאות  ועל  דא איקרי רזא פלא ואת אלף סלקא הכא נהרא
פלא אות  פלאות  והא  אוקימנא וכל אילין סמכין אבל |
אילין רתיכין  דקאמרן  כד  סלקא ה"א בתראה אתקשר באת
ו"ו אינון רתיכאן דיליה פרישאן על נוקבא כדקאמרן וכל
| אינון רתיכאן  דלא  כלילאן  באינון  רתיכין  עילאין
595  כולהו סחרן סחרנהא דנוקבא רזא דא כד נוקבא לא אתקשרת
| בדכורא  חפייא  לה חד קליפה תקיפא דסתים נהורא וכד
אתקשרת בדכורא חפיין לה כל הני רתיכין עילאין ותתאין
| אינון  קליפה קדישא דחפיין לה ואתלבשת בהו ואתקשרת
באת ו"ו עילאה בה"א דנקודה עילאה סתים בגווה וכד איהי
600 | נטלה לון  וכולהו בה כדין אתעבידו כולהו כגוונא דא

581 דמאן | ס ק מאן / בשבילין ואורחין | ס ק אורחין
ושבילין / 585 כלל | ק לכל / 586 ומאי(1&2) | ס ק ומאן /
588 באת... דקיימ' | ק חסר. / ה"י | ס ה"א / קדמאה | ס
חסר. / 590 רזא | ס ק [דא] / נהרא | ס ק והכא / 591 אבל |
ס ק וכל / 593 רתיכאן | ס ק רתיכין / 594 רתיכאן | ס ק
רתיכין / 595 סחרן | ס ק חפיין/ 598 ואתלבשת | ק ואתלבשה
ואתקשרת | ס ק והיא אתקשרת / 599 עילאה(1) | ס עילא ק
נטלא עילא / דנקודה | ס ק די נקודה / 600 נטלה | ס ק נטלא

182

## ARAMAIC TEXT

כ) ואסתים נקודה עילאה דקיימא באמצעיתא ואיהו ו"ו |
דאזלא בעגולא למעבד גופא לאסתמא האי נקודה כגוונא
אחרא עביד גופא באינון רתיכין ואיהי נהורא דקיימ' |
באמצעיתא וכדין איקרי ה"א הכי נמי האי את רזא דו"ו
605 אינון גופא וקיימא ברזא דא והיא נקודה באמצעיתא |
ובגיני כך כולא חד והאי נקודה עילאה איקרי חכמה
עילאה והאי נקודה תתאה איקרי חכמה תתאה חכמה | זעירא
והאי ה"א בר דהאי נקודה אתרשים בקדמיתא בלחוד הא יוד
נקודה חד עילאה דקיימא על תשע סמכין | כמא דאוקימנא
610 ואילין לא איקרון בשמהן בר אילין ה"ו באינון רתיכין
דילהון אבל אינון ט' יו"ד נפקי מגו בוצינא |
ואתרשימו תחותוי דיו"ד ואינון תשע נקודין ואתפשטאן
בכל אתוון בגין דכל אתוון נפקין מן יו"ד הני נקודין
תשע | נפקין מתשע אינון ואע"ג דאמרן דהני תשע אינון
615 תחותוי דיו"ד עליה דיו"ד אינון אבל אינון סמכין לה
ואינון רתיכין לתשע | אוחרנין דאיהו רזא דאין סוף
וכולהו קיימין ליו"ד וכל הני דלתתא אסתימו ואתהדרו
להאי נקודה ועל דא כל יומין חסר כאן

601 ציור | ק חסר. / 603 רתיכין | ס ק [דילה] / נהורא | ס
ק נקודה / 604 האי | ס אית / 605 וההיא | ק והאי / 607
חכמה(2) | ס חסר. / 608 והאי ה"א | ס ב"פ / בלחוד הא | ס
ק בלחודהא / 609 תשע | ס ק תשעה / 610 אילין ה"ו | ק חסר.
/ 611 אינון | ס ק הני / ט' | ס ק תשעה / נפקי | ק דנפקי
/ בוצינא | ס בוציצא / 612 תשע | ק ט' / ואתפשטאן |
דאתפשטן / 613 יו"ד | ס ק [באלין שבילין דילה כמה דאתוון
נפקין מן יו"ד] / 614 מתשע אינון | ס ק מאינון תשע / 615
תחותוי | ס ק תחותיה / 616 לתשע | ק לט' / דאיהו | ס ק
דאינון / 617 קיימין | ס קיימן / ואתהדרו | ס ק ואהדרו /
618 ועל...כאן | ק חסר. / חסר כאן | ס חסר.

# INDEX

Anthropomorphism 21, 67
Aristotle 13, 44, 53, 70, 106
Authorship of the Zohar 4ff.
Balaam 28
Balance scale 66, 105
Body 66
*Book of Creation* 62, 69, 99, 105, 108, 109
Chariot 63, 108
Commandments 19
Corporeality 45
Creation 10, 16
Creative and providential forces 16, 17, 19, 20, 116
Cruelty 41, 42, 66
Descriptive terms 14, 108
Demiurge 36
Descriptive terms 65
Destroyer 40ff.
Dialectic 27, 30, 31, 49, 51, 53, 56, 65, 70, 116, 125, 140; dialectical balance between unity and opposition 52, 66, 118, 138; dialectical suppression of expression of Judgement 107; dialectical suppression of expression of Mercy 109
Divine actions 16, 22; attributes 7, 9, 10, 11, 12, 13, 14, 15, 17, 25, 27, 37, 44, 108, 130; attributes of action 11
Divine Anger 28, 42
Divine will 52, 101
*Dvekut* 12, 17, 20, 30
Dualism 36, 37, 40, 43
Elements 25, 69, 136
Empedocles 43, 44, 45, 46
Epistemology 47
Ethical dimension 116, 120, 126, 130ff., 138
Evil 29, 39, 43, 56, 57
Extremes 13, 14, 27, 30

Fire 138
Formal Causality 45
Gikatilia, Joseph 3, 4, 5, 7, 10, 13, 14, 15, 17, 18, 19, 20, 30, 31, 106, 108, 109
Gnosticism 6, 30, 142
God's *Ways* 9, 14, 15, 29
Gottlieb, Ephraim 4, 106, 108
Governance 19, 39
*Guide of the Perplexed* 12, 13, 14, 17,
Heavens 25
Hegel 47, 54
Heresy 27
Horizontal dimension 116, 122, 126, 132ff., 138
Human love 49, 51, 52; sexual love 44
Identity and difference 48
Idolatry 28, 29, 42
Image of God 21, 22
*Imitatio Dei* 11, 12, 13, 14, 20, 23, 30
Inclusion 70, 120
Ineffable 23
Infinite 121
Interpenetration 138
Jewish philosophy 3, 21
Judgement 14, 24, 25, 27, 28, 30, 36, 37, 39, 41, 43, 49, 52, 55, 116, 126, 130
Justice 27, 29, 30, 40
Kadari, M. Z. 105
Kindness 14, 24, 27, 30, 130
Knowledge 16, 20, 23, 31; indirect knowledge 54, 118
Law of non-contradiction 53, 139
Left 25, 26, 27, 62, 66, 126
Letters 51, 52
Levels 16
Liebes, Yehuda 98, 100, 101, 106
Light and darkness 138
Logical Principles 46, 47
Love and Strife 43, 44, 45, 46, 47, 123

# INDEX

Luria, Isaac 35, 54, 59
Magic 18
Maimonides 7, 8, 9, 10, 11, 12, 13, 14, 15, 16, 17, 19, 20, 27, 29, 43, 69
*Major Trends* 6, 7, 98, 108, 109
Mechilta 37, 38, 40, 41, 42, 66, 102
Medieval Jewish thought 6, 7, 23, 31
Mercy 14, 25, 27, 28, 29, 30, 36, 37, 43, 49, 52, 53, 55, 116, 126; collapse of Mercy and Judgement into each other 54; resolution of opposition 48, 49, 54, 56 58, 119; transcendence of limitation 49; reconciliation of finitude with the infinite 123
Microcosm 21
Middle path 14, 27
Middle side 68, 126
*Middot* 11, 14, 15, 16, 19, 20, 21, 22, 26, 30
Mishnah and Talmud 3, 11, 27, 46, 104, 110
*Mishneh Torah* 8, 13, 69, 107
Monotheism 42, 57
Moses 8, 9, 10, 11, 12, 29, 120
Moses de Leon 3, 4, 5, 7, 10, 15, 24
Mysticism 9, 12, 20, 24, 30
Myth 6, 42
Name 16, 17, 18, 21, 49, 53
Names 18, 19, 20, 61, 107, 130
Negation 47, 58, 124
Neo-Platonism 6, 44, 45
Ontology 47
Opposition 13, 39, 56, 68, 140; antithetical forces in God 30
Pantheism 57
Paradox 49, 51
Philosophy 43, 45
Prayer 10, 18, 20, 25, 28, 120

Predominance 70
Prophetic enlightenment 9, 12
Prosperity of the wicked 29
Providence 10, 13, 16, 17, 20, 42
Rabbinic theology, sources, etc. 7, 17, 27, 31, 35, 36, 41, 43, 45, 48, 57, 66
Right 25, 26, 27, 62, 66, 126
Scholem, Gershom 4, 5, 7, 23, 42, 97, 109
Sectarians 36
*Sefer HaBahir* 105
*Sephirot* 7, 14, 15, 16, 17, 20, 21, 22, 23, 24, 25, 30, 105, 108, 109, 129
*Shaare Orah* 4, 7, 13, 15, 17, 18, 19, 21, 22, 31, 48, 60, 61, 100, 101, 106, 109
*Shaare Tsedek* 4
Shechinah 29
*Shekel haKodesh* 7, 15, 17, 25, 26, 107
*Shoshan Eduth* 7, 15, 27
Side of holiness 57, 110
Side of impurity 57, 110
Speculative knowledge 8, 12
Spinoza 47
Spirituality 45
Study of Torah 18, 19
Suffering of the righteous 29
Support 63
Symbolism 6, 22, 23, 25, 35, 51, 52, 55; symbols of Opposition and Unity 65ff.; mathematical Symbols 62ff.; optical Symbolism 63ff.; orthographic Symbols 60ff.; tabernacle Symbolism 67ff.
Sweetening of Judgement 58, 133
Tabernacle 64
*Targum* 68, 102
*Ten Sephirot* 24
Theism 57

Theurgy 20
Thirteen attributes (*middot*) 11, 12, 105
Throne 22, 99
Tishbi, Isaiah 4, 98
Torah 18, 19, 21, 60
Transcendent Creator 52, 54, 55, 115
*Tsimtsum* 54, 56, 58
Unity of God 17, 36, 70
Vertical dimension 116, 122, 126ff., 138
Water 138
Work of the Chariot 22
Work of Creation 45

www.ingramcontent.com/pod-product-compliance
Lightning Source LLC
Chambersburg PA
CBHW022102160426
43198CB00008B/314